ATL
the education union
Published in
partnership
with ATL

Managing
Teacher
Workload

Edited by Nansi Ellis

First Published 2016

by John Catt Educational Ltd,
12 Deben Mill Business Centre,
Old Maltings Approach,
Melton, Woodbridge IP12 1BL

Tel: +44 (0) 1394 389850
Fax: +44 (0) 1394 386893
Email: enquiries@johncatt.com
Website: www.johncatt.com

ISBN: 978 1 909717893

Set and designed by
Theoria Design

Contents

Introduction

You've picked up this book because you really need to cut down your workload. You love teaching – the bits where you are actually teaching anyway. You came into this job to make a difference to children's lives; to engage young people in the thrill of understanding your cherished subject. You love that 'wow' moment when a concept becomes real, a skill becomes second nature; you want to support students to understand their unique identity and culture, to learn to live in the world we have, and to work to change it. You want to expand every pupil's horizons.

But you also want a life.

You'd like to be able to go home at night with the feeling of a job well done, rather than a truckload of books to mark. To spend some time thinking about how you can really engage that tricky class in this week's learning, rather than filling out another lesson plan. You'd like to go to work excited about the day ahead, knowing you will get to challenge yourself and be challenged to deepen your knowledge and skills, rather than spend your evening in another boring admin meeting. And, let's be honest, you'd quite like to enjoy some time with family and friends, or taking that belly-dancing class, or whatever it is, without feeling guilty.

You're not alone.

In a recent survey by ATL over 80% of those who responded said that workload pressures made them want to quit the profession in the next five years – a profession that they had joined with such high hopes. This is a desperate situation, and **Something** (as they say) **Must be Done**.

But how bad is it really? If you read the OECD's *Teaching and Learning in Schools* study (TALIS)[1], carried out in 2013, you'll find that teachers across all the participating countries work an average of 38 hours a week, with an average 19 of those hours spent teaching. England's teachers spend a similar amount of time teaching (something like 21 hours a week), but overall they work around 48 hours: ten hours a week more than the average. And according to the detailed report on England's teachers, one in ten work more than 65 hours a week. Teachers in England spend more of their working lives on activities other than teaching than they do on teaching. How does this compare with your hours?

What are teachers doing in those hours? Again, the data proves very interesting.

---

1   You can read all the reports from TALIS 2013 here: www.oecd.org/edu/school/talis-publications-and-documents.htm

In England, almost eight of those hours are spent planning and preparing lessons; six hours are spent marking and around four on 'general admin' (other work includes meeting with parents and offering extra-curricular activities). 82% of teachers report that they provide written feedback on children's work frequently or nearly always, compared with an average (among the high performing countries) of 47%. Teachers in England spend far more time on planning lessons and on marking than many other countries. And I was surprised by the figures in ATL's survey, carried out in 2015[2], that put meetings and emails high on the list of workload burdens. Again, you might like to think about how your working pattern compares.

We have a pretty good idea what causes this busy work. Government and its agencies must take a large part of the blame: continual change of curriculum and assessment means that teachers can't use last year's work as a basis for this year; changes come late, so that teachers and leaders must rewrite plans and change timetables to accommodate them; fear of inspection leads to a focus on processes (especially writing everything down) instead of effective practices. Many of the chapters in this book identify these pressures.

The speed of this change is also a problem, with politicians looking for quick and simple fixes, rather than long-term support for education and the profession.

And, there are things that you may be doing that increase your own workload. Do you plan lessons by yourself even when others are teaching the same subjects or age groups? Do you collate and create your own resources, even when there are good quality resources available elsewhere? Are you required to produce a level of detail, or a consistency of approach in marking or planning that's unnecessary for teaching and learning? If you are a leader, does your practice contribute to workload for your colleagues?

Too often, school cultures can be more about compliance than collaboration or creativity.

Does it have to be like this? No. Again, the TALIS figures show that five of the highest performing systems have average teacher working weeks of under 40 hours. In Finland, teachers spend only five hours preparing lessons and three hours marking (half of what teachers in England spend).

One of the interesting locations within the TALIS data is Shanghai. Not for the reasons usually cited, about pedagogy or curriculum, but because of their focus on professional development. In the TALIS survey, Shanghai teachers reported spending 29 days in the previous year on courses and workshops (the average is

---

2   www.atl.org.uk/about-time-workload-campaign/workload-and-you/work-life-issues.asp

nine hours)[3]. Although they spend only 14 hours a week teaching, their working hours are high, with eight hours spent on marking and eight on planning. But much of their planning is done collaboratively: they meet regularly (often weekly) in scheduled groups to discuss best practices, to share advice and to create common lesson plans. Their professional development is embedded in their jobs, with time spent observing each other's lessons in order to learn from more experienced teachers, or to mentor less experienced ones. In addition to this, new teachers are expected to spend 120 hours on professional development in their first year, and then 360 hours every five years; 'senior level' teachers are expected to spend 540 hours every five years.

This isn't necessarily the answer for England's teachers, and we must be wary of 'policy tourism': picking the bits we like from a system without acknowledging the different cultures and expectations which will have an impact. It definitely isn't a recipe for reducing workload. But it does raise the question of whether we should prioritise our time better. And it invites us to consider what we really want.

How can this book help?

Each of the following chapters explores different aspects of workload. Some are very practical; others are personal reflections on how a school, or an individual, are addressing workload from different perspectives. Many of the chapters end with questions for reflection, to help you in your own journey to reduce workload while focussing on what's important.

The first two chapters focus on the workload working groups set up by the DfE in response to the workload challenge. Nansi Ellis explains their key messages, while Mary Myatt draws out practical ideas for school leaders reluctant to take risks.

The next chapters offer ways of addressing workload through initial teacher training (Joe Pardoe), through curriculum and assessment change in a primary school (Lee Card), through behaviour management (Toby French) and in large scale curriculum change in a secondary school (Judith Vaughan). Within this section is also a quick guide to meetings, taken from ATL's workload campaign resources.

Heath Monk's chapter reflects on the importance of making time and creating the culture for genuine professional development, while Julian Stanley gives tips and techniques for managing your own stress and workload pressures. In between is a quick guide to marking.

The following chapters are much more specifically about monitoring and

---

3   www.oecd.org/edu/school/TALIS-2014-country-note-Shanghai.pdf

managing workload – as a leader in the interview with Robin Bevan, as teachers working together in Collette Bradford's chapter, and as the role of the Governing Board in Emma Knights' chapter. This is followed by a quick guide to data management.

The final chapter, from Mary Bousted, reminds us that the role of government must be about more than producing recommendations and guidance on workload. There is much that we can do individually and at school level to reduce workload. But national policy-making is at the heart of many of the workload problems that teachers and leaders face, and Mary suggests changes to the processes of policy-making and to the focus of government policy, if ministers are to fulfil their first duties of ensuring enough teachers join and remain in the profession.

What emerges clearly from these chapters is that workload, and the pressures it produces, can be better managed if schools are open, trusting and respectful. Schools with strong values and principles are better able to resist knee-jerk reactions to national change, and are more confident in developing practices that they know are right. Schools which include the whole community – leadership, teaching staff, support staff, pupils and parents – are better able to make changes that are sustainable, reducing workload down the line. And schools which prioritise professional and collaborative learning in order to strengthen the resolve, the knowledge, the skills and the creativity of the profession, are better able to stand up to a government that is focussed on quick fixes.

In truth, as many of the contributors acknowledge, these kinds of practices take many hours. But the best school leaders think about what work they can remove, before they introduce something new; they think about how to use time more wisely instead of asking people to spend more time. Confident teachers ask questions about practices; they evaluate their own impact and compare with others. And they work in schools where colleagues, including governors, do everything they can to carve out time for this kind of professional practice, by removing requirements for pointless busy work.

Although some of these chapters are written by leaders, or seem to be aimed at leaders, don't dismiss them if you don't have a formal leadership role. I hope they will provide food for thought and evidence to share with your leadership team.

None of these chapters are offered as examples of perfect practice. Their authors are describing journeys of possibilities. ATL doesn't endorse all or any of these ideas as solutions to your problems, and there may be practices outlined here that don't fit with your ideas, or mine either. But they are the ideas and experiences of your colleagues, teachers and leaders who work in education and have taken some time to reflect and draw out their thinking. We all learn better when we learn from each other.

The authors

Robin Bevan has been Headteacher at Southend High School for Boys since September 2007. Prior to that he was Deputy Headteacher at KEGS, Chelmsford and Head of Mathematics at Westcliff High School for Boys. He has a keen interest in educational research, and is devoted to 'bridging the divide' between academic research and classroom practice: he is chair of the National Teacher Research Panel, serves as an elected member of the National Executive of ATL, has been an active member of the EPPI (Evidence for Policy and Practice Information) research reviews, and was the 'classroom voice' of the Assessment and Learning Research Synthesis Group. He has a MEd in assessment and curriculum issues, and a PhD from the University of Cambridge, establishing the importance of peer dialogue in the effective use of ICT, and illustrating the powerful relationships between feedback and motivation. Robin is a passionate cyclist, and holds several local championship titles.

Dr Mary Bousted is general secretary of ATL and AMiE. Mary represents the interests of her members to the government, and to a wide variety of other stakeholders. She contributes regular articles for newspapers and education journals, including an extremely popular blog for the TES, and appears frequently on national media. She is also an accomplished public speaker. Mary previously worked in higher education at the University of York, Edge Hill University and at Kingston University where she was Head of the School of Education. Prior to this Mary was a Head of English, and an English teacher in comprehensive schools in North London. You can follow Mary on Twitter – @MaryBoustedATL

Collette Bradford is director of organising at ATL. She leads a team which works directly with ATL members in all sectors of education, and she works closely with ATL Future, a member group which encourages and supports new professionals to work together for a better future for education. Collette began her career in law; she has first-hand experience of union activism having held roles of workplace and corporate site rep for a finance union and has studied leadership at Leeds Beckett University. Collette has worked in trade union recruitment, organising and development for over 16 years. She has special interests in distributed leadership, relational organising and union renewal. You can follow Collette on Twitter – @ColletteATL

Lee Card is Deputy Head at Cherry Orchard Primary School in Worcester, and a Specialist Leader of Education for CPD, curriculum and assessment. He has taught in Herefordshire and Worcestershire schools for 12 years, eight of these as a Deputy Head. Lee has led whole-school curriculum developments in two schools, currently at Cherry Orchard, where the innovative approaches undertaken have been showcased as a case study in ATL's 'A Curriculum That Counts' initiative[4]. Lee has written for ATL's member magazines and has commented for the *TES* and *The Guardian*. He sees the growing use of social media as a vital CPD tool for teachers and leaders and attributes much of the work being undertaken in his setting to a developing 'research-led' ethos. Lee led a workshop on Assessment Workload through the Twitter-inspired groundswell event, #LearningFirst. You can follow Lee on Twitter – @eduCardtion

Nansi Ellis is ATL's assistant general secretary for policy. She leads the development of ATL policy, and she and her team liaise with stakeholders, using policy to negotiate, influence and challenge government policy. She focuses policy development in ways that support sustained member activity. Nansi believes that if education is to change for the benefit of children and young people, then those who work in education need to take a lead, and the union must support them to do so. She began her teaching career as a primary teacher in a bilingual school in west Wales, and then moved to London to teach in a middle school. She worked at the School Curriculum and Assessment Authority, and then the Qualifications and Curriculum Authority, helping to develop the early years foundation stage, before joining ATL as primary education adviser. You can follow Nansi on Twitter – @ATLNansi

Toby French is a history teacher based in south Devon. Teaching in some very challenging schools, he very quickly realised that behaviour management was perhaps the most important aspect of both a teacher's practice and a school's culture. He blogs at mrhistoire.com, for which he has been nominated as the *TES*'s teacher blogger of the year. His book, *Show and Tell*, will be released this year by John Catt Educational. You can find him tweeting at @mrhistoire

Emma Knights is Chief Executive of the National Governors' Association (NGA), the leading charity for guidance, research, advice and training for school governors, trustees and clerks. Prior to her appointment in 2010 she was joint CEO of the Daycare Trust. Before that, she worked in a number of roles in the voluntary sector, including the Legal Services Commission, Citizens Advice and the Local Government Association. As well as leading projects on child poverty,

---

4   acurriculumthatcounts.org.uk

early years and educational attainment, Emma has written on a wide range of topics and is co-author of the NGA's *Chair's Handbook*. Emma regularly addresses legislators and the media on governance issues, as well as conferences of school governors, trustees, clerks and school leaders. She was a governor at her children's secondary school in Warwickshire for seven years and in 2015 became a founding trustee of the Foundation for Leadership in Education. Follow Emma on Twitter @NGAMedia

Heath Monk has spent eight successful years as Chief Executive of The Future Leaders Trust, which he led from a small start-up to its present position as an established and highly regarded leadership charity. As well as creating more than 160 new headteachers, the Trust is notable for its recent work in designing and delivering Executive Educators, a development programme for those leading Multi Academy Trusts. Heath has worked in education for more than twenty years, first as a secondary school teacher and later at the Department for Education, where his roles included Deputy Director for Workforce Reform (in which role he oversaw the development and delivery of the National Workforce Agreement) and (the first) Deputy Schools Commissioner for England. You can follow Heath on Twitter @Heath_Monk

Mary Myatt is an education adviser. She works in schools talking to pupils, teachers and leaders about learning, leadership and the curriculum. She maintains that there are no quick fixes and that great outcomes for pupils are not achieved through tick boxes. She is the author of *High Challenge, Low Threat* and is a TEDx speaker. You can follow Mary on Twitter @marymyatt

After graduating university in Politics and History, **Joe Pardoe's** first taste of education was through the JET (Japanese Exhange of Teachers) Programme. Working on a small island off the coast of Nagasaki, he worked with the local board of education to deliver a language and culture curriculum to 40 elementary and junior high schools. He realised that he wanted to work in education, so to develop his understanding further, he worked in schools in Shanghai, China as an English teacher. He returned to the UK and joined the Teach First programme in 2011, teaching History in a school in Hull. He is currently Head of Humanities and Project Based Learning at School 21, Newham, London. You can follow Joe on Twitter – @historypardoe

Julian Stanley is the Chief Executive of Education Support Partnership[5] (formerly the Teacher Support Network), the leading UK charity providing health and wellbeing support services for training, serving and retired staff in the education sector. Over 30,000 individuals contact Education Support

---

5   www.educationsupportpartnership.org.uk, phone 08000 562 561, or text 07909 341229

Partnership every year. The charity offers a 24/7 helpline, practical and emotional support, expert advice, telephone counselling, money advice and a welfare grants programme. They also provide training and workshops for leadership and staff across the education sector. Julian engages with policy makers, education leaders, teaching staff and governors to share the data collected by Education Support which illuminates some of main causes of stress and common mental health problems. He also writes a fortnightly column in *SecEd*. Julian believes the damage of stress can be prevented, and that the impact of the current recruitment and retention crisis can in part be eased through the development of trust, collaborative and supportive cultures, continuous professional development & by enhancing the status of the profession. He has previously worked in civil service, local government, the arts, community and economic regeneration as well as in education.

Judith Vaughan graduated from Exeter University in 1995 and taught Maths in three schools around the country before settling in Sheffield to take up the post of Head of Maths at High Storrs School in 2002. Judith then became Assistant Head overseeing the use of data and the curriculum, before becoming Deputy Head in 2013 with responsibility for Curriculum and Assessment. In recent years, when any school leader must be expert at managing change, Judith has challenged and supported the High Storrs staff through significant curriculum, assessment and qualification reform. Much curriculum development has been imposed on schools, but High Storrs has succeeded in retaining its unique character by creating its own flexible and innovative approach to curriculum design.

ATL has been running a workload campaign for members since November 2015. We have developed a workload tracker and a range of factsheets and guidance. Members and others have been actively involved in our twitter campaign #make1change.

All materials are freely available on ATL's website www.atl.org.uk/abouttime

What to do about workload: the government's response

Nansi Ellis, ATL

Towards the end of the coalition government, Nicky Morgan (then Secretary of State for Education) and Nick Clegg (then Deputy Prime Minister) finally realised that workload was a problem for people working in schools. And so they set a 'workload challenge', inviting the profession to let them know what kinds of tasks were taking so much time, and why those tasks were being done at all. 44,000 responses later, Ministers had learnt that most teachers identified similar tasks as being unnecessary, too detailed or too frequent: data management, marking and lesson planning. Those were closely followed by basic admin tasks, staff meetings, reporting pupil progress and implementing new initiatives.

The reason for much of this workload? Accountability and the perceived pressures of Ofsted, and tasks set by middle leaders. Not far behind those two comes policy change at national level.

Government responded with a few more initiatives. It committed to carrying out regular surveys of workload, to see if it was getting better. It issued a 'protocol', commonly believed to mean that any national changes would have at least a year's lead in time[6]. And it set up three working groups to look at the top three workload burdens: marking, data management and planning.

The groups were made up of practising teachers and school leaders, along with union representatives, Ofsted, DfE and experts in each field. They were given some hints about what they might look at (deep marking was one, textbooks another), and tasked with identifying recommendations for reducing workload. I was involved in the group looking at planning and teaching resources and I was struck by the commitment of those involved, many of whom were travelling

---

6 Actually, the protocol refers only to 'significant changes to accountability, the curriculum and qualifications'. And the 'lead in times' refer to initiatives in those areas coming from the Department which require schools to make significant changes which will have an impact on staff workload. So for example, the Department would publish subject content and Ofqual would publish its assessment requirements for any new qualifications at least a year in advance of first teaching (with accredited specifications and additional materials to follow later). This means that the crazy business of planning for GCSE teaching from September when specifications are only accredited by March fits within this protocol. Following pressure from the unions, the government is currently reviewing this protocol.

long distances to attend meetings, willing to read papers given to us and to share resources and research of their own, and passionate about supporting colleagues to reduce time spent on pointless activities. But we realised very early on that reducing overall workload is extremely difficult: effective planning takes a lot of time. So we tried to focus on reducing the pointless parts – writing it all down, lesson by lesson; handing in individual lesson plans and seating plans; trawling the internet for the perfect resource – or spending hours creating your own.

We spent a lot of time talking about why people do these things – and I know the other groups did too. Why do school leaders feel it necessary to collect in weekly planning, or to carry out booklooks and issue verbal feedback stampers, or to collect test data on a half-termly basis? A lot of this we put down to the pressures of accountability: leaders need to be sure that effective planning is happening, that feedback is being given, that pupils are progressing – and having it written down means you can prove it, to Ofsted, to governors, to whoever asks. But why do teachers feel bad about using textbooks, or other people's lesson plans? Where does a requirement for three-colour marking come from?

Reports[7] from the groups came out during the Easter holidays in 2016 – and I shall refrain from any comment on the irony of that. They aren't perfect, but they are an important addition to resources for reducing workload. They are important because they imply two key messages: that we are all agents of change, and there are things we can do now to make changes; and government has an important role to play in reducing the burdens it places on teachers and leaders.

The three reports were accompanied by a letter to the Secretary of State (then Nicky Morgan), which very clearly sets out responsibilities for her, the Government and its agencies. Specifically, it calls on her to maintain the commitment to removing unnecessary workload; to give greater attention to the pace of national change so that reforms don't place excessive demands on teachers and schools leaders; and to trust the dedication, creativity and professionalism of teachers and leaders. The Secretary of State accepted all recommendations.

We are all agents of change

The workload reports make a number of key recommendations. These are not checklists of activities you should or shouldn't do; but they do embody some clear principles:

---

7 www.gov.uk/government/publications/reducing-teachers-workload/reducing-teachers-workload

· Marking should be meaningful, manageable and motivating;

· Planning is a process, not the production of written plans;

· Data collection must have a purpose, and the amount collected should be proportionate to its usefulness.

There are recommendations for practice which include:

Marking:

· Review current practice to ensure marking is meaningful, manageable and motivating;

· Evaluate the time implications of any whole school marking and assessment policy for all teachers;

· Monitor marking practice (collaboratively) and evaluate its effectiveness on pupil progress;

· Develop a range of assessment techniques

Planning and resources:

· Review demands made on teachers in relation to planning;

· Don't automatically require the same planning format across the school;

· Ensure that a fully resourced, collaboratively produced, scheme of work is in place for all teachers for the start of each term;

· Make clear who will be planning new schemes of work, and make sure they have time to do so;

· Ensure high quality resources are available, both professionally produced and created in-house;

· Engage in collaborative planning, developing skills and sharing expertise;

· Consider the use of externally produced and quality assured resources

Data management:

· Collect data that are purposeful, valid and reliable;

· Stop collecting data if the burden of collection outweighs their use;

· Do not routinely collect formative assessment data;

- Summative data should not normally be collected more than three times a year per pupil;
- Implement an assessment and data management calendar in order to understand assessment demands throughout the school year;
- If you don't understand why data is being collected, ask.

Some of these recommendations are aimed at school leaders, governing bodies, local authorities and Multi-Academy Trusts (MATs). Others are aimed at teachers. School leaders or teachers should feel free to use these recommendations to begin the process of change. If you want to reduce workload, these reports could be a good place to start.

Government and its agencies have responsibilities for change

It's important that some of the recommendations are also aimed at government and its agencies. Ofsted was involved in all of the groups, and DfE officials were actively engaged in the discussions. Knowing that the recommendations are endorsed by these groups is important, as it gives them credence: it's always useful to be able to point to an official document to back up your claims that 'Ofsted doesn't need this'.

Messages from Ofsted:

Ofsted does not expect performance and pupil-tracking data to be presented in a particular format;

Ofsted does not expect to see any specific frequency, type or volume of marking and feedback, nor any written record of oral feedback;

Ofsted does not require schools to provide individual lesson plans to inspectors, nor previous lesson plans.

In accepting the recommendations, Ofsted has committed to continuing to communicate those messages; to monitor inspection reports to ensure no particular methods of planning, marking or data collection are praised as exemplars; and to emphasise these commitments in the training of inspectors.

The DfE has made important commitments too. All groups recommended that the DfE disseminates the messages and principles through its system leaders, including Regional Schools Commissioners. The data group made recommendations with regard to releasing data early enough so that schools don't have to duplicate, and reducing the number of log-ins schools need in order to access and share information with the DfE.

In the planning group, we made specific recommendations that:

- DfE and its agencies should commit to sufficient lead in times for changes for which the sector will have to undertake significant planning to implement. This includes releasing relevant materials in good time.
- DfE should review the DfE protocol to ensure it is fit for purpose, and takes full regard of the workload implications of any change.

And the messages in the Chairs' letter[8] to the Secretary of State are powerful:

'greater attention should be given to the pace of national change...'

'an initiative enacted without sufficient time for schools to understand, plan and work with the changes runs the risk of being poorly implemented... it has a broader impact on the functioning of the system, on recruitment and retention, and on the morale of the profession.'

'...your continued championing of the ability for schools to make decisions that suit the needs of their pupils is essential'

In her response, the Secretary of State is clear:

"You quite rightly point out that action needs to be taken by all parts of the education system – from practice in the classroom to policy set at Westminster. For my part, I commit to rise to the challenge you have rightly set Government."

The profession's response

Some have complained that the workload reports and recommendations are 'motherhood and applepie', setting out a host of ideas that no-one could argue with, but with no real plan to reduce workload. Remembering that the working groups were made up of teachers and leaders, from across the sectors, it's important to take these recommendations in the spirit in which they are intended – these are not directives from on high, but suggestions for consideration from others in the profession. Some will work in your situation, others might work if you can work with other schools, and yet others may prove

---

8 www.gov.uk/government/publications/letters-from-the-teacher-workload-review-groups-and-nicky-morgan

impossible in the circumstances, but all are worth reflecting on.

What is important is taking some kind of action. That could be action at school level, in your own classroom or with your colleagues to address an issue throughout the school. But it's also vital to keep an eye on whether the government and its agencies are fulfilling their end of the bargain. Have you seen an Ofsted report recently which praises a particular method of marking? Challenge it: write to Ofsted and point it out. Are different people asking for data in different formats? Challenge them: explain how your format suits your needs and invite them to use the format you use.

The Secretary of State has committed to 'rise to the challenge' of championing schools' ability to make decisions that suit the needs of pupils. Many of the following chapters set out how teachers, leaders and schools have worked to do exactly that, while also being mindful of workload. Be inspired to start your own journey, and to share your journey with colleagues.

Take-away

We are all agents of change; government also has responsibilities to reduce workload.

Questions

Where will you start, to tackle your workload?

The Big Picture on workload

Mary Myatt

This chapter urges leaders to consider their overarching strategy, vision and culture in order to do things differently. Nobody has deliberately set out to increase workload. But increased it has. So what can senior leaders do to address the drivers for this and how can they find ways of cutting through anything which is not absolutely necessary? This chapter explores further the three main strands identified in the Government's Workload Challenge, set out in the previous chapter: planning and resources, data management and marking.

Planning

First, to planning. It is essential for leaders to have conversations with colleagues about the difference between 'lesson planning' and 'lesson plans'. Planning is critical and is fundamental in providing the structure and architecture for pupils' learning. Results are better when teachers are given time to plan together on a scheme. These should identify the 'what' and the 'why' of the content to be taught.

Best practice in planning starts with an overarching question, ideas for opening up the content and the things to be taught over the medium term. These constitute the big picture and framework for what is to be taught (Judith Vaughan's chapter gives a practical example of this in a secondary school, Lee Card's chapter gives an example in a primary school). They are the roadmap. This is a useful metaphor for thinking about the curriculum to be taught. A roadmap shows the destination, but provides a number of routes to get there. This allows for teachers' autonomy in the delivery of the scheme as it unfolds, lesson by lesson. When good quality schemes of work are in place, they should reduce teacher workload.

The Department for Education's workload review group on planning and resources[9] identified planning a sequence of lessons as more important than writing individual lesson plans. So what leaders could do to support this aspect of the workload challenge is to stop asking for detailed daily lesson plans, if that is current practice. The only situation where daily lesson plans might be

---

9 www.gov.uk/government/publications/reducing-teacher-workload-planning-and-resources-group-report

an expectation is when senior leaders are supporting a colleague via coaching. Here, precise planning might be needed to improve practice, in which case the plans should be prepared jointly with the senior leader as coach, as part of the larger scheme of work.

The most compelling reason for moving away from compulsory daily lesson plans is that not only are they not necessary, they can get in the way of the bigger 'flow' of the sequence of learning. As leaders, this might appear risky.

So, let's be clear about why it might not be risky to do away with daily lesson plans. First of all, what do lesson plans tell senior leaders that they don't already know? If they have an overview and indeed have had some input into some of the longer-term plans, they do not need a detailed lesson plan to tell them this. If they are honest, how many leaders read the individual lesson plans from every teacher? In a school with ten teachers and five lessons a day that would be about 250 plans to check; with 100 teachers, 2500 to check. Each week. Are any senior leaders doing this, seriously? And if they are, wouldn't the time be better spent going in to the actual lessons to see how things are going? Not as lesson observations, or learning walks, but simply by walking about. And offering support if needed and affirmation for work well done. How much more powerful this would be, than reading all those plans, which often bear little relation to what is happening in the classroom.

Second, senior leaders might deem it too risky to do away with lesson plans because they believe that they might be needed for an inspection. Ofsted has made it clear, in its 'mythbusting' document for schools[10], that they do not expect to see lesson plans, only evidence of planning. Apart from anything else, time is so tight on an inspection that there wouldn't be time to read files of lesson plans.

The only thing which inspections comment on is impact – the impact of the delivery of curriculum plans on children's learning. It would be technically possible to have perfect plans, which do not translate into meaningful practice for children in the classroom. And the danger of this is that it is possible to be seduced into thinking that the piece of paper is the work, when in fact it is the action in the classroom which is the work.

Third, senior leaders might believe it is risky to stop insisting on lesson plans as they will have less control and view of quality assurance. But this is like a restaurant checking that all the orders have been placed so that dishes can be prepared. It suggests that the paperwork is more important than the meals

---

10 www.gov.uk/government/uploads/system/uploads/attachment_data/file/463242/ Ofsted_inspections_clarification_for_schools.pdf

that eventually end up in the restaurant. Any decent restaurant will check on the final product, and tweak it to make it better, rather than thinking that the process stops at the ordering. So, for those leaders reluctant to let go of the safety net of lesson plans, they might want to trial it for half a term. Then check what difference it makes not having them. Those schools which have done this have found that the quality of teaching and learning in the classroom goes up, not down. It is a case of fewer things, done in greater depth.

Given the above, one of the recommendations in the working group's report[11] is that 'senior leaders should consider the cost benefit of creating larger blocks of time for this practice to make the planning activity as productive as possible and reduce the amount of time spent by individual teachers on individual planning.' As John Hattie says:

'planning can be done in many ways, but the most powerful is when teachers work together to develop plans, develop common understandings of what is worth teaching, collaborate on understanding their beliefs of challenge and progress, and work together to evaluate the impact of their planning on student outcome'.[12]

Data management

Now, to the workload related to collecting data in schools. This is the advice from the Report of the Workload Review Group on data management[13]:

'leaders and teachers should challenge themselves on what data will be useful and for what purpose and then collect the minimum amount of data required to help them evaluate how they are doing.'

The move away from levels should help with this. The advice from the DfE's Commission on Assessment Without Levels report[14] is that key performance indicators are the most efficient way forward. In other words, schools should identify the key ideas and concepts which are taught, and whether pupils have understood and have grasped these. The vital word here is 'key': not every aspect of what is being taught, but the big concepts and ideas only. It is not possible to evidence everything, so schools should not be seduced into thinking

---

11 www.gov.uk/government/uploads/system/uploads/attachment_data/file/511257/ Eliminating-unnecessary-workload-around-planning-and-teaching-resources.pdf

12 Hattie J (2012) 'Visible Learning for Teachers, Maximising Impact on Learning, pages 67-74.'

13 www.gov.uk/government/uploads/system/uploads/attachment_data/file/511258/ Eliminating-unnecessary-workload-associated-with-data-management.pdf

14 www.gov.uk/government/publications/commission-on-assessment-without-levels-final-report

that this is possible. The right sort of evidence tells a big story about what pupils are able to do. (Emma Knights' chapter on governance points out that these principles should be welcomed and supported by governing boards.)

Leaders should keep in mind that the most robust evidence of progress and attainment is what pupils produce and say about what they have learnt. This is why their work, including written work as well as how they articulate their learning, provide the best insights into how well they are doing. Some schools are using tools like SOLO taxonomy[15] to capture whether children's learning is surface, deep or conceptual.

Leaders need to hold in the forefront of their thinking that the data or information is a symbol for what pupils know, understand and can do. Any data collection is meaningless if this relationship is not made, checked and moderated.

or example, an inspection team will ask school leaders how well pupils currently in the school are achieving. They will look at any system which the school is using to capture this. Then they will ask to see children's work and to talk to children about their learning, to gauge whether the information or data collected is in line with what the children are saying and producing. The key question is: is the work done by children broadly at age related expectations? And if it is not, how are leaders and teachers using this information to close the gaps in learning?

One of the problems sometimes seen in schools is that investments are made in commercial tracking systems, which are very similar to old levels. They create a false impression of what pupils can actually do and in some cases they drive how the curriculum is delivered. This is completely the wrong way round. School leaders and teachers need to agree what is to be taught and then work out the simplest way of capturing this. Otherwise, commercial packages drive the learning, rather than the other way round.

Some schools, like the Wroxham School[16] keep their tracking to the minimum. Instead, they have regular, high quality conversations with pupils and parents about what they are doing well and where they still need to develop. Pupils, in discussion with their teachers, identify key pieces of work which show what they are capable of. These are used to share with parents and anyone else who needs to know.

It helps everyone if there is a timetable for data or information collection, together with a rationale for its frequency. In this way, all those involved in its input and analysis are clear about what is expected of them and why.

---

15   See for example: pamhook.com/solo-taxonomy/

16   thewroxham.org.uk/our-school/assessment/

Marking

And finally, to marking. The report of the workload review group on marking[17] acknowledges that *'marking is a vital element of teaching, but when it is ineffective it can be demoralising and a waste of time for teachers and pupils alike.'* So the critical thing for leaders is to make sure that it is effective.

What are the key principles which senior leaders need to consider here? First, that quality always trumps quantity. There is no link between the quantity of marking and pupils' progress. At its worst, teachers write extensive comments on children's work and children do nothing with the feedback provided. This is a complete and utter waste of time. Wise leaders are describing how marking fits into the bigger agenda of feedback. Feedback is information and advice, whether verbal or written, which improves a child's learning. Leaders discuss with colleagues the purpose of high quality verbal feedback. And together they explore how powerful this can be. Then, they agree what high quality, purposeful written feedback looks like. This is linked closely to curriculum planning.

In depth feedback might only be needed at the end of a significant piece of work, because most of the feedback will have been verbal and given in a number of lessons, leading up to a final piece of work. Leaders talk through why anyone would feel the need to have a verbal feedback stamp. Why would anyone use these? A waste of time and ink. And above all, they consider the main audience for the feedback. It is for the child, not the adult.

As a result, there should be no more cries of 'Should I be marking every piece of work?' Why on earth would you, when most of it is redundant. A leader's role in this is to have some big conversations around a few simple themes: What would happen if we didn't mark at all? If we are going to mark, who is the main beneficiary? How much of this should be done during the lesson? What would it look like if we limited marking to just a few pieces of work?

Tom Sherrington has written a very careful analysis of what high quality marking and feedback looks like[18]. The grid at the bottom of his blog post shows how teachers might do less, more effectively. While it is written with secondary colleagues in mind, it is a useful talking point for colleagues working in all phases. Joe Kirby has analysed marking which is maximum impact, minimum effort[19]. As identified above, much of this takes place in the classroom, because

---

17 www.gov.uk/government/uploads/system/uploads/attachment_data/file/511256/
    Eliminating-unnecessary-workload-around-marking.pdf

18 headguruteacher.com/2012/11/10/mak-feedback-count-close-the-gap/

19 pragmaticreform.wordpress.com/2015/10/31/marking-is-a-hornet/

that is where the learning takes place. Feedback should be as close as possible to the action. And Dylan Wiliam has thought and written more than anyone else on what meaningful, effective feedback looks like.[20] Any of these would be very good starters for a discussion about marking less and doing it really, really well.

To summarise, in all these elements affecting the workload challenge, there is a simple line running through and it is this: fewer things, done in greater depth, produce better results. The job for senior leaders is to set aside the time, in professional development time and elsewhere, to begin the conversation.

Take-away

Fewer things, done in greater depth, produce better results.

Questions

Are there things that you do, or are requested/required to do, that seem pointless? Have you asked why they are done?

Which of these three issues cause the most workload in your school? Use the tools in Collette Bradford's chapter to analyse this and plan to change it.

---

20 www.ascd.org/publications/educational-leadership/apr16/vol73/num07/The-Secret-of-Effective-Feedback.aspx

How can we solve workload problems of those just starting out in teaching?

Joe Pardoe

I recently stood watching a student who I have known since she was 11, now 16, deliver an excellent speech and answer audience questions with confident ease. I couldn't have been more proud of her. I recently stood on the sunny school playground while the students played football and had seemingly random and interesting conversations with students who stopped to tell me about their weekends. I recently saw a student sing and perform in a school musical and was honoured to think that I have played a part, however small, in this student's life. I genuinely believe that teaching is one of the best and most noble jobs in the world.

It can be easily forgotten, but we should remind ourselves more often that schools are undoubtedly exciting and inspiring places to work. We should remember the numerous times in a day students and colleagues make us laugh. We should remember the music concerts, drama performances and art exhibitions in which students surprise us with their brilliance. We should remind ourselves that being a part of a child's life is a privilege and honour – how many jobs in the world allow us to help shape and develop a child and watch as he or she grows into adulthood? We should remember the 'thank-yous' from grateful students and parents, the hardworking student who gets the results they absolutely deserve and the emails from students who have gone on to get a place in university or the job that they really want. I could go on.

I once heard Vanessa Ogden, a hugely successful headteacher, give a speech in which she implored the audience, mostly non-teachers, to get into teaching. Her passionate plea concluded *there is no better working environment than classrooms*. Schools are the crucible in which culture and civilisation is created. Who would not want to be a teacher?

However this is only part of the story. Teaching is undoubtedly a stressful and high pressure job. This is highlighted by the statistics; there is simultaneously a shortage of teachers nationally and an increasing number of teachers leaving the profession. Stress and workload is, sadly, one of the top reasons cited for leaving classroom teaching[21]. As much as I love teaching, it is impossible to

---

21 See for example ATL's survey of members, in which over 80% of respondents said that they had thought about leaving the profession because of their workload.

deny there are many things which can cause enormous amounts of stress and worry. We are trying our hardest to deliver lessons, plan lessons, mark work, attend meetings, speak to parents and deal with colleagues. While there are many ways teachers, schools and government can, and should, reduce the unnecessary pressure on teachers, we should also confront head on the fact that teaching will always be a stressful job. Any profession which deals with humans and emotion will put enormous pressure on individuals. However, Initial Teacher Training could play an important role in improving the wellbeing of teachers.

Light at the end of the tunnel?

A key component in solving this problem is not only reducing stress and workload pressures but also developing strategies to deal and cope with the inevitable pressure teachers will face in the course of carrying out the job. I was lucky enough to have some fantastic, and realistic, mentors during my early years of teaching. As I naively once explained my new strategy for dealing with workload, one of my mentors (a teacher of 20 years) explained to me that I should stop looking for the light at the end of the tunnel, and instead learn to enjoy living in the tunnel.

He also brought up Parkinson's Law that work expands to fill the time available for its completion. This advice made me realise that I should not only focus on reducing the stress, workload and pressure I face, I should also focus on strategies for coping and dealing with the pressure that I face.

This chapter will focus on both of these aspects and explore some of the ways teacher training routes and schools can better prepare and support new teachers in reducing their workload and stress, while also dealing more effectively with the inevitable stresses and pressures of the job. However, before exploring these tools, techniques and strategies, it is important to look at the role ITT could play in leading the change, rather than simply coping with it.

New Thinking: Initial Teacher Training as a driver of change

Albert Einstein once said (apparently), *"we cannot solve our problems with the same thinking that created them"*. In my experience of teacher training, we were encouraged to work long hours to reflect the demands of the job. This is fine for some, not fine for others. We all have different views about what constitutes a positive work life balance, which is a good thing; being told to work long hours as a blanket statement is not. In addition, teacher training routes, in an attempt to help prepare teachers for the stresses they may face, may actually be contributing to the problem.

As a career changer, I was shocked to hear on my teacher training route how stressful the job will be and how many 'valleys of despair' I would pass through, without any techniques to get out of them (other than wait for it to pass!). Yes, teaching is a stressful profession, but in my opinion it is no more uniquely stressful than other professions which deal with humans.

Simply talking about how stressful the job can be doesn't prepare someone for dealing or coping with the stress. Instead, it presents as the norm that the profession is uniquely stressful and you should expect to have periods of self-doubt and worry. This can lead to new teachers seeing worry and stress as normal and something that they are helpless to influence. Feeling helpless in situations is one of the biggest causes of stress.

This means that ITT, in whatever form it takes in the future, should be looking to train teachers not only to reduce their own workload and provide strategies for dealing with the pressures of the job, but also to instil a sense of duty that, as a profession, we should be doing more to improve the wellbeing of educators and reducing workload pressures. This would mean that over a long period of time, we will be developing leaders who are proactively improving the wellbeing of teachers in schools and looking for ways to reduce workload. ITT should also play a part in training people to help reduce this stress. It should actively encourage trainee teachers to take a stand.

Knowledge and a new tool-kit

In order to take a stand, ITT should focus on mental and physical health as well as teaching practice and pedagogy. As the physical and mental wellbeing of pupils creeps into the national agenda (and rightly so), so too should this happen for teachers.

In order for teachers to properly help the wellbeing of students, they must be proficient in the techniques themselves. Identification of the problem is one of the first things teacher training routes should consider, to give people the tools to deal with and, crucially, help to reduce the problem. Just as many strive to increase focus on developing subject knowledge, ITT should focus on developing understanding of what causes stress, tension and anxiety and how to remedy this. Julian Stanley's chapter gives more practical ideas.

Therefore, alongside subject knowledge sessions and training about pedagogy, trainee teachers should also be given access to the growing body of knowledge about improving wellbeing and reducing stress. These could be simple techniques which have been shown to increase wellbeing, such as:

- 'Three positives'
- Writing letters of gratitude
- Mindfulness exercises
- Diet
- Physical activity
- Understanding of the physiology of 'happiness'
- Priority matrices
- Checklists

Many of these ideas come from the work of Dr Martin Seligman (see, for example, Flourish[22]; Authentic Happiness[23]; or Learned Optimism[24]).

These types of exercise will allow teachers to regain an element of control when things do become challenging. It should be presented that looking after your own mental health while teaching is as important as knowing the pedagogy and having subject knowledge. The profession simply cannot sustain itself with the number of teachers leaving due to stress. All those who are in the profession know that teachers model and set the tone of their classroom; in my experience, happier and more relaxed teachers create a happier and more relaxed attitude in the classroom, leading to more effective learning.

However, hearing about these techniques in lectures is not enough. Knowledge without application has very little effect, and as soon as we become overwhelmed by events the learning can soon disappear. Like learning to swim, it is better to do the learning in the pool rather than focusing purely on the theory. Therefore it is vital that these tools are built into the 'on the job' training element through reflection.

Reflection for coping

Many teacher training routes include trainee teachers keeping a 'reflective journal' to reflect on practice. This is, at present, mostly based around teaching and learning and very little focus is placed on personal wellbeing or longevity. The reflection process could be improved to encourage more thought about things such as sleep, diet, physical health and mental wellbeing. Not only would

---

22 Seligman, M (2011) Flourish: a new understanding of happiness and wellbeing Nicholas Brealey Publishing

23 Seligman, M (2003) Authentic Happiness Nicholas Brealey Publishing

24 Seligman, M (reprinted 2006) Learned Optimism: How to change your mind and your life Vintage Books USA;

these have the short term effect of forcing new teachers to consider these aspects, it would, over a longer period help to put physical and mental health high on the agenda when it comes to training new teachers.

These methods, both increasing the knowledge of wellbeing and then applying this knowledge on the job, will help new teachers to cope with the demands and stresses of the job. However, education often contains many unnecessary pressures and ITT has a duty to train teachers to spot these activities and encourage them to change their own practice and those of the school more widely. To identify this 'waste' it might be useful to turn to businesses, specifically manufacturers, who have made reducing waste a key priority for many years.

Kaizen – reflection for efficiency

Many studies have shown the huge effect skilful reflection can have on driving improvements. Toyota is known as one of the world's most productive manufacturers. For a long time, during the 80s, it was the biggest and most successful car manufacturer in the world. While there were many contextual reasons for Toyota's success, one thing that emerged as a key driver of their success was the constant reflective look at what work adds value to the end product – *kaizen* or 'continuous improvement'[25]. In Toyota's case, the end product is profit, in our case, the end product is the education the children receive.

Reflection on practice is, rightly, a key factor in ITT. However, a missing component is not just how effective something is, but how long that thing took to prepare and what was sacrificed in order to make it happen. In other words, how much value do our actions have on the learning in a classroom, and which actions in our day do we do which do not add as much value, and which can therefore be reduced or cut out completely.

Reflection structures should be added to increase the amount of time new teachers reflect on these things, with increased focus on the longer term and broader picture, rather than just individual lessons or activities. For example, I spent a long time in my early days as a teacher cutting up materials, putting cards in envelopes and creating differentiated worksheets. These were all effective (to varying degrees) but, on reflection, they were simply not worth the effort.

Working long hours is not the same as being productive and everything I chose to do, meant I chose *not to do something else*. My reflection was never structured to support me in considering what was sacrificed vs the impact on learning.

25 Womack, James P (2007) The Machine that Changed the World Simon & Schuster UK

Learning suffered over the long term due to a focus on the short term. Trainee teachers should be encouraged to constantly look to find ways of improving their practice, not just in terms of narrow outcomes for one class or group, but for efficiency. This should form, for example, one of the key components of lesson observation feedback.

This new form of reflection and feedback would also help to shift thinking away from the short term and more to the long term – this is something I believe is a key factor in high levels of stress in the teaching profession. In order to move to long term, rather than short term thinking, ITT needs to put more emphasis on effort vs effectiveness.

At the height of the Cold War, Eisenhower's Secretary of Defence, Charlie Wilson was posed with the problem of maintaining the US military dominance while also constraining debilitating costs. He, famously, ordered his staff to focus on giving him "more bang for the buck!" We are in a crisis in which we have a shortage of resources and we need to focus, as a profession, on how to get the most effective learning while dealing with busy timetables and numerous pressures.

Learner not teacher – the 'lazy' teacher[26]

We need more 'bang for our buck', ways of conserving our resources, and one of these ways is to focus ITT much more explicitly on the learner not the teacher. Ofsted is, rightly, moving away from a focus on what the teacher does in a lesson to focus much more on learning over a longer period of time. We should be much better trained to think about what the students are doing in lessons and less about what we are doing or have done in preparation. Over-preparation can lead to over-focus on activities which take a long time to prepare but have little relative impact, while under-preparation often leads to teacher domination in lessons.

The fact is, the students should be doing most of the work in lessons and not the teacher. Good, effective planning should 'free-up' the teacher. There are numerous tools and techniques for shifting the balance from teacher to student and again, lesson observations should focus on student activity, not teacher actions or activity. This shift, from a focus on the teacher to a focus on the student is a key component of improving the wellbeing of teachers.

Shifting the focus allows us to put our activities into context, and this is something experienced teachers have practised doing. All teachers, but most

---

26 The title is taken from Smith, J (2010) The Lazy Teacher's Handbook: How your students learn more when you teach less Crown House Publishing

importantly new teachers, need also to be able to put individual lessons into context and ITT has an important role in ensuring this is the case. Think about these questions:

· What was your most powerful learning experience? Why?
· What is your strongest memory of school?

Time is a river of passing events

When, inevitably, things do go wrong it is important to put the event in context. This can be very difficult in the current climate, where teachers and the teaching profession have been oversold the importance of their short term actions. We have been told that we can have a huge impact on a child's life and that every second of learning in the classroom counts. We have been bombarded with research and theory telling us how to make the 'perfect lesson'. This can create a situation where we over emphasise the importance of one activity or one lesson. Therefore, when something does not go to plan or a student is 'off task' we can put enormous pressure on ourselves and overestimate the negative impact this will have on a child's learning experience.

The reality is, the long term school experience improves a child's life chances far more than one 'hero' teacher's self-sacrifice. The old adage 'consistently good is outstanding' should form the basis of ITT. One of the key causes of teacher stress is the feeling of time pressure – many new teachers feel that there is not enough time to do a 'good enough job'. There is enough time if you see yourself as a part in a process – this process involves much more than just your lesson or your subject.

Thinking back to the questions posed earlier, I actually remember very little from my school days. My most powerful learning experiences did not occur in classrooms. I certainly do not remember lesson objectives, films, posters, textbooks, card sorts or any of the things many teachers spend a lot of their time preparing or worrying about.

The teacher I remember the most was a supply teacher who taught me for one month. He didn't teach me any history, but he broadened my horizons and showed me that a student from any background can travel the world. He started a chain of events which led me to university and to working abroad.

Another teacher, who made us work from a textbook and whose lessons I remember as quite boring gave me the confidence, through informal conversations, to believe I could achieve. Most of all, it was my parents and family who had high expectations of me which led to me achieving at school and feeling content with my life but always looking to learn and grow.

Put simply, teachers and students look through different lenses and there is no such thing as a universally 'good' or 'effective' teacher. The things we worry about might quickly disappear from memory and the throw away comments might last a life time. We should constantly be striving to improve and develop our skills and knowledge, but in doing so we should expect things to go wrong. When things do go wrong (the sign of a developing teacher) we should be encouraged to put things into perspective and not beat ourselves up over something which, in the grand scheme of things, is not important. See Heath Monk's chapter on CPD for more on continually learning, and the freedom to take risks.

Conclusion

Great teachers are those who are constantly self-reflective and understand that their actions have consequences, but they are able to put these consequences into perspective. Great teachers are those who understand that they are a part of a learning journey, not the *only* or the *most important* part of the journey.

How can teacher training support new teachers to reduce workload? I think it should be improved in four main ways:

1. It should focus on leading a change.

ITT should lead the way in developing cohorts of teachers who understand that their mental and physical wellbeing is as important as their subject knowledge and pedagogical understanding. If this does not happen, the profession will not be able to sustain itself. The toothpaste tube has been squeezed dry – it is time to stop squeezing and instead look to change.

2. It should provide knowledge about wellbeing.

ITT has a duty to increase understanding of mental, physical and creative wellbeing. Teachers are role-models to students and it is no surprise that student stress has risen at the same time as teacher stress. If we wish to improve the wellbeing of our young people, and we should, then we should make improving the wellbeing of teachers our priority.

3. ITT needs to structure reflection to focus on wellbeing.

Knowledge is important but is easily forgotten when the job actually starts. Therefore it is important that the reflection element of teacher training is reformed to focus on not only coping with the pressures of the job, but also reducing less effective work.

4. Context and perspective.

ITT needs to move away from the focus on individual lessons and activities and help new teachers to focus on the long term development of our students. School should be about providing memorable experiences today, not simply preparing students to sit exams in the future. The lesson that goes wrong, if properly reflected upon, is a positive thing in the long term and will have no, or very little, negative impact on students. The stressed and overwhelmed teacher who shouts at a class will have more of a negative impact compared to the relaxed teacher who learns from mistakes.

As Marcus Aurelius wrote: time is a sort of a river of passing events, and strong is its current; no sooner is a thing brought to sight than it is swept away and another takes its place, and this too will soon be swept away.

Reflect and move on. It probably was not as important as you think.

Take-away

Plan for the long term, aim to be consistently good; reflect on your practice and on your choices, thinking particularly about the balance of workload and impact.

Questions:

Do you find opportunities to reflect on your own wellbeing and strategies to support this? Can you find a mentor or buddy to help?

When you reflect on your practice, do you also consider how long it took to prepare and whether the outcome was worth the time?

Do you consider what you chose not to do, and what the impact was of those choices?

Does lesson observation in your school encourage this long term *kaizen* reflection?

Who does most of the work in your lessons (and in preparation for those lessons) – you, or the students?

Designing a sustainable curriculum and assessment system

Lee Card

The Workload Challenge is important in demonstrating that workload, particularly that associated with marking, data management and planning, is being taken seriously by government. But we need to be realistic about what the government has the ability to influence. As Michael Tidd says,

> 'The reality is that the DfE had tasked itself with a mission of improving something that it really couldn't control...The sad truth for teachers is that the vast majority of the excessive workload we suffer is caused by school leaders, trying to dance to the tune of an inadequate and inconsistent inspectorate.'[27]

We have been asked to 'step up' as a profession; so let us then step up *for* our professionalism. Let us stand up for, and as, school leaders and teachers, leading with trust, with autonomy and within a collaborative school-led system that WE drive with our own ideology – that of pedagogy. In this chapter, I will reflect on what I see as a tangible example of this as the staff and community at Cherry Orchard Primary School (COPS) took the macro change of the National Curriculum 2014 and used it as a vehicle to drive our own, deeper, micro changes to curriculum and, subsequently, assessment design. During the process of this, we discovered over-arching principles required to ensure that changes we made supported the workload challenge for teachers and led to a sustainable and iterative process of development.

Challenging The Curriculum: Challenging Change

I believe that the curriculum is everything. Everything you do, say, offer, suggest, present, question, experience and feel is the curriculum. Dylan Wiliam put it far better than me at the SSAT 2nd Curriculum Conference (July 2014): The National Curriculum is the intended curriculum which then gives rise to the implemented curriculum. Neither are the real or enacted curriculum, the daily lived experience of young people in classrooms; at the enacted level curriculum is pedagogy.

How many schools, I wonder, actually know what their school curriculum is?

---

27 michaelt1979.wordpress.com/2015/02/06/the-challenge-for-the-dfe-with-workload

How many schools are blindly stumbling from one National Curriculum to the next, ripping up each prior document and chuntering about everything changing? To paraphrase Wiliam again, it's one of the greatest tragedies of the last 20-odd years that school leaders have assumed the curriculum is a non-issue because the government has decided what the curriculum should be. Over four academic years, we have whirred in a process of seemingly continual change; not just changing our curriculum but also challenging our perceptions of what curriculum and assessment *are* and *mean* in our school.

Change generates workload. It can also heighten stress and even ignite a fear of change itself. Values can, and should, inform the change; when there is a real sense of moral purpose as a driver then school leaders have the crucial 'software' in place before moving onto the 'hardware' of actual design[28]. I have witnessed this myself through teachers' varying reactions to developments and the perceived implications for their workloads. Where teaching staff have been involved in, empowered by and passionate about the process, I have seen them react favourably to the outcomes, even when the actual workload implication for them is the same or greater than before the change. Conversely, where teachers feel that change hasn't been managed or implemented in this way, even a tangible reduction in actual tasks and activities can still be perceived as adding to their workload.

Jim Collins' idea of defining a value proposition in his book, *Good to Great*[29], supported our process. He suggested that the answers to the following three questions create a value proposition:

· What are we passionate about?
· What are we 'best' at?
· What drives our engine?

Whilst we didn't necessarily answer these questions directly, I see much of this rationale when I reflect on the process as a whole. At Cherry Orchard, our curriculum change had a few core principles which were intrinsic to its development and will be crucial to its sustainability. Over the past twelve months, we have embraced the three driving principles of a *Learning Without Limits*[30] ethos championed by Dame Alison Peacock: 'Trust, Co-Agency, Everybody'. It is interesting to me that these resonate within our practice back in 2013.

---

28 Descriptions feature in the AMiE publication by Mark Wright (2015) Restructuring in colleges, schools and academies, handling change with care at amie.atl.org.uk/Images/restructuring-in-colleges.pdf

29 Collins J (2001) Good to Great USA: William Collins

30 learningwithoutlimits.educ.cam.ac.uk

i) Vision (trust): A clear 'big picture' that the School Curriculum is the embodiment of everything you offer within a school and that it incorporates the National Curriculum;

ii) Ownership & investment (co-agency): All stakeholders are involved in the process and thus take a vested interest and ownership in the product from the outset. This also ensures that the end product is fit for your community's needs.

iii) A shared language (everybody): For us, this was having a set of clear rhetoric for impact – the Three Rs (Reality, Relevance and Rigour) and our school aims, which have become the bedrock for everything we strive for. When we have truly embedded this into our school community, the aims will be like letters through a stick of rock in everyone and everything we do, from planning documents and Governors' meetings to assembly themes and pupil dialogue.

These principles might be seen as a blueprint for all change which is supportive of workload implications if approached with a morality mindset. Indeed, we used the same principles when approaching our change from National Curriculum Levels to an assessment system without levels which I will refer to later in the chapter.

Parts of the Process: Principles into Practice

What follows is a broad chronology of the stages of curriculum change at Cherry Orchard; where appropriate, they draw upon the three principles highlighted previously and offer practical examples of how these were played out in our school.

The idea that most great learning happens in groups should not be lost on school leaders; collaboration really is the stuff of growth and is the vehicle for '*Ownership & Investment*'. This ethos provided the initial platform for curriculum change at Cherry Orchard and also underpinned many of the parts of the process of that change over time. Collaborative approaches can also distribute workload and maximise time allocated to a process of change, namely meetings. There were several ways in which we utilised this principle across a range of key voices:

· **Efficiency Through Sharing** model of information gathering regarding teaching and learning. The Headteacher planned, delivered and reflected collaboratively on lessons across the school in a 'Learning Study' rather than 'Lesson Observation' model. The reports were then read through as teams over staff meetings to support the drawing of key findings.

- **Lesson Study** model of collaborative planning and teaching. Initially structured to support information gathering on engagement within the curriculum. Now a driver for CPD across the school.
- **School Council** as a pupil forum for reflection on teaching and learning. The title 'What helps me learn best?' as a half-term project saw around 600 pupil voices synthesised into some key messages for our future curriculum: *"Please make my learning meaningful, suited to my needs and could you wrap it up in something that makes me really want to find out more?"*

At this early stage, all pupils and staff had enjoyed some input in the discussions around teaching and learning. A crucial component in building trust, however, is that the voice is listened to and, where deemed most effective, acted upon. In this way, co-agency becomes lived-out and true ownership and investment is harnessed. It was affirming when my colleagues and I presented a slide containing only the three letter Rs to a full staff in September 2013; they were able to create the three terms we had suggested behind the scenes over the summer holidays: 'Reality, Relevance and Rigour' based on their shared experiences to date.

A *shared language* was starting to be created and, most powerfully, was being created by the teachers themselves, not by a small group of senior leaders sitting in a room conjuring mission statements and slogans using the latest education buzzwords. However, we were clear from the outset that we recognised the anxieties that teachers would feel about curriculum change. We looked to allay this quickly in a few ways:

(i) Make a clear statement of intent that we wanted to avoid onerous workloads. We placed this question to staff in one of the initial curriculum staff meetings: *"How do we get an exciting and engaging 21st century curriculum without creating huge amounts of work?"*

(ii) Afford time, space and, dare I say it, minimum lead in times for significant changes. We presented this by stating: *'We don't begin actual change until Spring 2014, using the Autumn Term to prepare'*

(iii) Focusing in on the principles Jim Collins described, namely what are we passionate about and what are we best at. We presented this by stating: *We centre our work on the 'COPS School Curriculum Aims' and make the new National Curriculum work for us* (we were passionate about this) and *We keep the excellence and we re-model the average* (we believed we were already doing some great stuff in our classrooms).

(iv) One thing I have often found with significant change is that we teachers struggle to 'see' how the changes will affect our day-to-day jobs. This isn't surprising given the inflated and distracting language often used around changes to educational systems. We tried to allay this by creating a short video parody based on the BBC's *Waterloo Road*. Stereotypical teacher characters went through the issues we thought our teaching staff would be feeling: the thought of having to re-plan everything; the fear of tight deadlines; a more narrow National Curriculum; having to find 'real audiences'; ensuring we covered the statutory elements of the National Curriculum. It was designed to be a bit of fun but it also demonstrated how real professional discussions might go and we mocked up some planning documents that the characters were supposedly looking at.

When reflecting a few years on, it is difficult to perhaps pin down exactly when the *vision* was truly born into a tangible, defined 'thing'. There were a great many smaller, almost incidental, elements – be they meetings, emails, or discussions in corridors that were parts of the bigger process. However, in that spirit of collaboration, and in the current climate of a school-led system (whatever that will come to mean), we were fortunate that national changes coincided around the time that I could enjoy quiet Saturday afternoons in Herefordshire with a humble, paperback book written by Geoff Rutherford, Headteacher at The Wyche School in Malvern. If any one document could be said to have made the most impact on our development, then *The Wyche Curriculum*[31] would be it. Most of the following processes were born out of the work Geoff and his team had conducted and that he had written about and generously provided for me to read.

Now writing in 2016, our *shared language*, or rhetoric, has almost reached words-through-a-stick-of-rock status. If we ask ourselves, as leaders of the school, why this is, I think we can point to one key, and increasingly common, attribute: *ownership and investment – everybody*. We unashamedly copied The Wyche's idea of generating a list of skills, attributes and qualities around one simple question:

> *"What is it you want the school to have given the children when they leave in Year 6?" Some years later the QCA used a similar question "What are you trying to achieve?" in their curriculum development tool; The Big Picture. Such questions remain the key feature in all good curriculum planning, drawing out the foundational issue of a school's ethos and values and allowing it to then ascertain how their own curriculum can be modified to deliver them.'* (Rutherford, G: 2012)

Our manifestation of this process worked as follows:

- Collating the views of governors, parents and staff on the key question above. Sharing the respective responses with each group and formulating

---

31 Rutherford, G (2012) The Wyche Curriculum – designing a curriculum for the 21st century England, Little Inky Fingers

an initial draft list of 'School Aims' where views overlapped, drawing them into categories: ours were *Learning, Self, Relationships* and *Situations* (since renamed *Attitudes*);

· A staff meeting split into three 'workshops' one of which was entitled 'How can we start to exemplify our school aims so that we might be able to assess pupils against them?' Some great ideas came from this collaborative, low-threat approach including the idea to develop simple definitions / school-based sentences to describe each aim;

· Two further staff meetings in which the wording, tone, presentation and planned profile of the Aims were given time and space to be thrashed out. It is worth noting that, during this term, we operated a 'reactive' staff meeting approach. This enabled us to build on from the energy and enthusiasm immediately, something we have not always had the chance to do when meetings are scheduled months in advance. It also kept the *vision* constantly in focus, with each iteration contextualised within the bigger picture.

· Integrating the School Aims, which by now were agreed upon as the core driver for our curriculum, into the planning documentation which would ensure their profile was great enough. Again, this was a consultative and collaborative process and, again, was as much about allaying fear and anxiety as it was about pushing the envelope of change. Teachers were supported toward a new system of collaborative 'outline plans' which they would then 'pitch' (another idea taken from The Wyche) to senior leaders of the school with assurances that:

(i) We weren't looking for a raft of new medium term planning documents – many of our teachers had been through various incarnations of re-writing plans and this wasn't the way to engender investment or trust in the process. We offered a few possible templates or suggested that they might have a better idea for how the layout should work – after all, it is the 5-day-a-week teacher who needs these documents to work for them;

(ii) We weren't holding the 'Pitch' meetings in order to schedule a punitive scrutiny of their planning;

(iii) We were starting with the assumption that we are already doing a lot of great stuff so the angle instead was to look to build on that and re-model anything that wasn't as brilliant;

(iv) This was a trial year in which staff would always have the safety net of falling back on their old planning if it wasn't working – a high challenge, low stakes approach.

(v) There was no need for us to re-invent the wheel. Schools should not be afraid of pre-designed documentation, from planning templates to textbooks, and these are messages that have been reaffirmed in the latest workload reports from the DfE's reporting groups. We were happy to issue staff with the Long Term Planning 'Jigsaw' documents designed by Michael Tidd[32] in order to free their own time to work on their pitch plans.

(vi) Again, time and resources were allocated to support the process, with staff teams released from class together to plan their 'pitches'. We have since written these into INSET days.

As a result of these processes, we now have a very clearly defined School Curriculum with the School Aims becoming more and more integral to school life. From the actual fabric and displays of the school buildings (the Year 6 pupils this year undertook a half-term project with a photography company to encapsulate our aims in images, and these now run the full length of the school hall and are in every assembly and newsletter) to the rhetoric in planning meetings, Governors' discussions and the wording used in pupils' learning logs and end of year reports to parents; by factoring in workload considerations and just good change-management processes, we have built something powerful, sustainable and, our original desire, future-proof to any national agenda.

Principles Are Practice

John Tomsett, Headteacher at Huntington School in York and author of *This Much I Know About Love Over Fear*[33], often quotes Tom Bentley in saying:

'Change your structures to accommodate your core purpose, rather than contort your core purpose to fit within your existing structures.'

If you wish to engender trust and credibility in any change process and, in doing so, protect workload, this is a great yardstick to work to.

Throughout this chapter, I have used the term 'principles' rather loosely and as a general term for 'a thing that we did in order to achieve something'. However, this is disingenuous. Having worked through two full processes with the community of our school – that of curriculum and assessment revolution and convolution – I can now reflect with the clarity that hindsight affords and conclude that it is only through the defining, approving and articulating of principles that we can claim any kind of positive change has been made. In the same way Dylan Wiliam describes the enacted curriculum as the point in which

32 michaelt1979.wordpress.com/2014/05/08/primary-curriculum-jigsaws-editable-template/

33 Tomsett, J (2015) This much I know about love over fear Crown House Publishing

curriculum is pedagogy, for me the 'enacted profession' is the point at which principles are practice. There are two fundamental definitions of the term 'principle' that resonate in this belief:

basic assumption: an important underlying law or assumption required in a system of thought;

ethical standard: a standard of moral or ethical decision-making.

The practical processes of change for our School Curriculum were driven by two demonstrable sets of principles at Cherry Orchard:

(i) The Three Rs – Reality, Relevance and Rigour;

(ii) The School Aims.

Embracing the community in the ownership, investment and co-agency of these principles created the *trust* required to render 'workload', as an issue or barrier to progress, negligible. Ensuring these principles are practice requires daily reflection and analysis of our actions; a good example of where we feel we have achieved this was during a recent Subject Leadership restructure. In a moment of blinding clarity, we moved from an unproductive thrashing around of ideas for what we wanted from subject leader job descriptions to a simple three-point document, driven by our Three Rs; changing our structures to fit our core purpose.

Assessment

We took the same 'principled approach' to our Assessment process, spending a full term to discuss then finalise our 'Principles of Assessment' with *everybody* a contributor toward the final outcome:

Cherry Orchard Primary School Principles of Assessment

The objective of our assessment system is to improve pupils' development.

Assessment:

- · *Is a picture of personal development and academic progress.*
- · *Is an on-going, diagnostic process involving children and informing teachers' practice.*
- · *Identifies what children can do and what their next steps are.*

Establishing from the outset what our basic assumption and ethical standards were, it became a much simpler process from there on in. We had a clear frame of reference for all decisions we had to make which we had all signed up to, unequivocally. We had established a metric of morality that ensured we could all hold ourselves to account with a shared and passionate interest in working to achieve an end goal that married with our principles.

Here are the steps we took from this point and how our Principles of Assessment drove the process.

(i) We allocated consecutive time slots to the process. Four staff meetings were planned in which:

- Staff year group teams were allocated one of seven pre-defined Assessment Systems on the education 'market' at that point. The leg work of finding these was removed from staff workload. (Note: All support staff and teaching assistants are encouraged to attend staff meetings and are paid for their time to do so – this is a small but significant aspect of establishing everybody's voice);
- Two full staff meetings were set aside for staff teams to research the 'big idea' behind these systems and create simple presentations;
- A Presentations Meeting allowed year group teams to evaluate the system being presented against the school's Principles of Assessment document;
- An Evaluation & Reflections Meeting ensured ALL feedback could be heard and recorded. This created a 'Research Outcomes' document which drew out the consistent elements of the systems evaluated that staff valued and felt were commensurate with our own Principles.

(ii) A proposed solution to our Assessment system research was offered to all staff. They were offered the chance to view the prospective system and formulate any questions that they would like answered before any agreement to progress was made. In receiving full answers to every question raised, not by email but in written form during a face-to-face and scheduled staff meeting, the importance of their role in the process was illustrated clearly. Genuine, purposeful and professional dialogue led to a much more structured outcome for school leaders. Indeed, this procedure enabled us to then create a seven-point action plan.

(iii) The seven-point action plan was then put to all staff to rank in order of their priority as front-line users of the system. This ranking system was shared explicitly with everyone and next steps were then clear and written into the next series of scheduled staff meeting time.

(iv) In the Summer of 2015, we had one staff meeting remaining that was pre-scheduled for Assessment. As is evident, consultation has presented itself as another crucial element in supporting workload concerns – so long as the consultative tasks are not onerous in themselves. Rather than make a top-down decision on the focus of this meeting, we asked the staff "What do you need from the final staff meeting in order for it to be most effective for your assessment practice come September?"

(v) Moving into this academic year, we have attempted to support workload concerns by listening to the practical day-to-day issues that present themselves when implementing anything new. Staff have told us what they need to make it work and we, as school leaders, have trusted their judgement and tried to facilitate their needs.

As a result:

- Each phase team gets designated release time, which will now be scheduled the full year in advance, from the whole-school assembly. This is valuable professional time to plan, moderate and discuss assessments collaboratively across two year groups;

- We use Twitter to regularly raise the profile of principled messages coming from Ofsted, particularly their National Director for Education, Sean Harford, and other schools around the country. A self-affirming boost of moral purpose works wonders for workload worries!

- INSET days are planned to focus on the principles and the moral vision as well as supporting tasks and processes that can be more effective in collaboration than isolation. As an example, our next INSET day will involve a healthy dose of moral alignment with two nationally-acclaimed speakers, both of whom will then work with our staff on two of our core development points including some moderation for Year 2 and Year 6 staff to support and alleviate their natural anxieties at this time.

- As our principles are born out of pedagogy, professionalism and experience, we are able to illustrate that much of the 'workload' teachers currently value is, or can be, deeply effective in translating them. Ostensibly, what works for the teachers will work for our pupils if supported and allowed to grow amidst a culture of professional dialogue. There is nothing more poisonous to a teacher's workload than the disconnect between what they value doing as a professional and what they are forced to do (see Heath Monk's chapter for more on the balance between 'compulsion' and 'craftsmanship'). Assessment and marking procedures are two domains that have clearly fallen foul of poor management practice in many schools over the past year.

In February 2015, as part of the panel in one of ATL's pre-election debates on education issues, I was heard to utter "The Curriculum is everything and everything is Assessment." These were broadly paraphrased ideas from Dylan

Wiliam and Chris Chivers respectively. It is remarkable to me that in the space of just two academic years, the teaching profession has been asked to change everything, with fundamental changes to both curriculum and assessment still ongoing today. Unremarkably, for many the implications on their workload and work-life balance have seen them leave the profession.

We haven't got everything right at Cherry Orchard and it would be disingenuous to suggest that every member of our team has skipped along merrily with a vastly reduced workload! However, by managing the processes of change through a principled approach, with a clear moral purpose and incorporating trust, co-agency and everybody as key drivers, we might well be workload neutral... perhaps even better.

Productive, useful work feels better than unproductive, useless work even if it takes a similar amount of time. [34]

Take-away:

Focus on one change at a time. Give time to reflect and embed.

Collaboration can distribute workload and maximise time.

A change that's focussed on your principles should stand the test of time.

Questions:

Do you know the aims and principles of your school – do they run through everything?

Are your staff meetings planned as a sequence to give time for background work and for reflection, discussion and decision?

Do you have opportunities to tell your leaders what you need to make a change work? Do your leaders facilitate those needs?

Do you draw on what others have done? What blogs do you follow? What books have you read?

Are you free to use and adapt other's resources, frameworks, planning documents to make time to make changes?

Is there scheduled time for staff to collaborate? How well is that time protected?

---

34 leadinglearner.me/2016/03/30/workload-and-the-blind-man

A quick guide to meetings

(taken from ATL's workload campaign)

What's the problem:

There are too many

They're not relevant and they wander off the point

Everybody has to be there, and they're just used to give information

"I've sometimes gone in on my day off for 'essential' meetings that then turn out to be something different"

Should meetings be held at all?

Meetings can be notorious time wasters. Held on a routine basis – whether weekly, bi-monthly or monthly – they are often tedious and wasteful. A meeting should only be held when it's the best way to achieve an objective.

Be clear about those objectives before you hold a meeting – are there better ways to meet those objectives? It's even more important to ask these questions before calling all-staff meetings. It's easy for these to become a habit, rather than a practice that meets everyone's needs.

What does good practice look like?

Effective meetings have clear agendas, which state the purpose of each item. All those who are affected by or have a part to play in the items (and **only** those people) should be present at these meetings. Meetings have opportunities to discuss and collaborate – they should not be about presenting information, as that can be done in other ways. Effective meetings have a time limit on each agenda item, so that all who are present have a responsibility to keep to time. Actions are agreed and circulated promptly, and then followed up.

Review your meetings

To review your current meetings, ask others and yourself:

- What do we want to achieve at this meeting? Are the objectives clear and, at the meeting end, have they been achieved?
- What do we want to achieve after the meeting is over?

- Could those objectives be achieved in a more efficient way *eg* imparting of information?
- Is the meeting necessary, or is it habit?
- What would happen if this meeting were not held?
- Who is needed – do I need to be at the meeting?
- Are all of these people needed all of the time?
- What percentage of the meeting was relevant to me?
- Could the meeting be held at a more convenient time?
- Could the meeting have been shorter?
- If it's a regular meeting, could it be held less often?

Once you've analysed your current meetings, here are some ideas to make sure the meetings you attend are as effective as possible.

1. Ensure objectives are clear

A meeting must have a specific and defined purpose. Meeting organisers should ensure all participants know and understand the meeting's objectives. As a participant, check the objective with the organiser. Sharing the objective with fellow attendees will support more highly focused meetings.

2. Should I be there?

Once you know the meeting objective, ask yourself if you should be there. When organising a meeting, it's worth taking time to think about who really needs to attend. When people feel what's being discussed isn't relevant to them, or that they lack the skills or expertise to be of assistance, they'll view their attendance at the meeting as a waste of time.

3. Sticking to the agenda

If you've been invited to a meeting, ask for the agenda. It should lay out the items to cover, along with a timeline of how many minutes will be spent on each item. An agenda keeps a meeting focused.

4. Start on time, end on time

If you have responsibility for running regular meetings, starting and ending promptly is important – people appreciate it when you understand that their time is valuable. Do not schedule any meetings for longer than an hour.

5. Should technology be in the room?

The reality is that if people are allowed to bring iPads or smartphones into the room, they won't be focusing on the meeting or contributing to it. As a participant, raise the issue if it's a problem in your meetings.

6. Follow up

It's quite common for people to come away from the same meeting with very different interpretations of what went on. To reduce this risk, the organiser can email the group within an agreed timeline after the meeting, highlighting what was accomplished. This should record the responsibilities given, tasks delegated, and any assigned deadlines. That way, everyone will be on the same page. As a participant, checking your understanding of meeting outcomes, either at the end or following the meeting, is a useful prompt for the organiser.

Reaping what we sow: why great behaviour should not mean more work

Toby French

Why does behaviour affect workload?

Whatever our ideological positions on the ultimate purposes of school may be, there's one thing the vast majority of teachers – and parents – will agree on, and that is that great behaviour is vital for children's success, whether academic or social. Yes, there will always be those we desperately try to avoid bumping into on the high-street lest they ostentatiously revel in their new found glory, all despite – or perhaps because of – that dreadful attitude they displayed to every other human-being in school ten years ago. "I must have been a nightmare to teach, Miss!", they snort. "I bet you're glad I'm not in your class anymore, Sir!", they chortle. "Oi, remember when you sent me out for being racist? Ha!"

But for the vast majority of our children success comes with hard work, confidence and a positive environment in which to learn. Because, y'know what? Children come to us to learn, about geometry and the medieval world, what Munch's screaming ghost might have feared and how to say *je t'aime*. But children also come to learn about how to be around others and survive and excel in society. Learning to behave well at school is vital for everyone, now and in the future, both inside the crumbling 1950s walls and down the local park.

And it's precisely because behaviour is so important that it needs to be at the heart and soul of any successful school. These schools are usually great at many things: often arts and PE provision is exceptional; there are clear links with both local feeder schools and the community as a whole; there's a camaraderie among staff. But there's one thing that every successful school has: great behavioural systems.

Unfortunately, many schools cannot decide what great behaviour is, insisting it is the result of great teaching and engaging lessons. In doing so, these schools place accountability for behaviour firmly at the feet of individual teachers, while removing any responsibility from the children themselves. Great behaviour, then, becomes an automated response to classroom magicians performing, as it were, for their customers.

But this view implies something else too, that great lessons mean systems don't need to be in place, or at least need not be rigorously enforced, because if behaviour's no good then it must be the teacher's fault. This surely can't be right? And if it is, well, we have a problem.

Schools which do not place the highest of values on the behaviour of their children, for whatever reason, cannot be said to be successful. And guess what? Their teachers are probably overworked from dealing with poor behaviour alone and unsupported. In these situations, in which I have worked, behavioural management really does take on that firefighting analogy, but a much more dangerous one than perhaps we imagine.

Take Mr Fudge. Mr Fudge is an experienced teacher, but has become fed up with the behaviour of certain children in 10Y. Knowing that the behaviour system in place is mired in bureaucracy, and that any email he sends will be passed between five administrative assistants who don't even work in the same office, he instead takes matters into his own hands. At the slightest whiff of Megan Obnoxious he begins to deliberately wind her up, knowing that she'll very quickly swear. Then he can send her out to wander the long, dark corridors of the soul while he gets on with some teaching. And while most of his remaining charges are delighted that Megan has been ejected into the vacuum, two others decide that they too would like to experience the true meaning of Zeno's anarchic state, and promptly push the big red button themselves.

But wait! These three young astronauts are now floating freely in the drama block and, devoid of space-suits and basic life-support systems, are knocking on doors, helpfully redecorating the toilets with loo-paper and texting their cosmonaut buddies in this marvellous co-operative atmosphere of mutual friendliness. "Oh for a simple system!" Mr Fudge whines later, as he fills out his ninth Intermediate-Level-Behavioural-Incident form, dropping tears onto the yellow-blue-green triplicates.

And what of Miss Juniper, the young languages NQT? She trained at a Catholic Girls' School, and once worked in one of those places where they expel you if you even squeak – what of her experiences with 9Q5 on Friday afternoons? Her poor Head of Department receives a minimum of twenty Minor-Nuisance-That-Doesn't-Really-Need-A-Departmental-Sanction-But-Just-In-Case-Ofsted-Look forms, such is her determination that every child shall succeed. But it's now March, and still not one of the Minor-Nuisancees has been sent out. And why? Because she's a Good teacher, and desperately does not want to be seen as needy, let alone lack evidence for pay progression. After all, she's been sitting in the staff-room at break, and whilst everyone agrees that Dylan Do-Nothing is annoying, that's "just the way he is." No-one else has any serious problems with him, and no-one else sends him out. Because it's more trouble than it's worth, and lesson plans have to be in next week, and "our kids are just chatty."

Poor behavioural systems create more work for teachers. They let children, their futures and communities down. And whilst we in schools cannot change societies on our own, we must surely stand tall in our insistence on certain moral absolutes: we are, at the very end, the last bastion of society and thus require the firmest of foundations.

Attitudes and expectations

Every school needs to recognise that the attitude it takes towards the behaviour of its children will directly affect the number of pupils and staff on roll, in terms of both recruitment and retention. Teachers at interviews very quickly make judgements of children's behaviour, albeit sometimes wrongly when the interview class is 7A*1. Parents, however, don't necessarily choose a school based on its behavioural reputation, at least not in terms of systems alone: there are walls, you see, and these can attempt to hide the worst of what lurks behind. Nonetheless, the behaviour of pupils is evident through proxies.

Take two extreme examples. 2,300-strong Endeavour High School has a shiny new, pre-BSF'd site, complete with one-to-one tablet provision, a towering glass library and a fish-tank in the dining hall. Advertisements are all over town, on buses and in the local paper. EHS has signed up to the European School Alliance, which means trips for the top-set Spanish class every year. It's proud of its partnerships with the local college and even had the Secretary of State down to visit the new music studio. EHS also, perhaps importantly, has a very low exclusion rate. The last Ofsted report gushed with praise for the teachers' use of Individual Education Plans, even going so far as to make EHS a case-study school for Outstanding behavioural practice.

Across town, though, is Discipline Academy, the boo-boys of popular opinion, you might think. With its dilapidated buildings and old-fashioned values (they don't even have a BYOD policy, the analogue-mugs!), DA is the school which the cool kids don't want to go to. What, they make you sing in public at Christmas? Pah! Look at them, the top-buttoned, long-tie'd, litter-picking, sport-winning losers! And there are also rumours about the scary teachers, excluding children all over the shop – their main drive is like a graveyard of broken futures.

But despite the glitz, EHS's results aren't much to speak of. Yes, they're an *insert-web-giant-here* Certified Education Palace, but they're finding it difficult to recruit teachers. And not only that, but their numbers are falling year on year. Parents are, strangely, choosing Discipline Academy. Why? Unlike DA, EHS's windows don't leak and they have a website that wouldn't look out of place as a display on the *Champs Élysées*. Beneath the glamorous façade, however, is a problem. Individual teachers are held accountable for behaviour, and pupils are not. Every night there are exhausted queues for the 'phones, SIMS crashes with increased pressure on the exhausted network and an exhausted couple who used to work in social services are running black-ops counselling sessions for the younger, exhausted teachers. There are rumours of a staff exodus this year, with three already having gained employment at the nearby dark place.

Senior management, though, clinging to their belief that the powers that be are interested in 100% differentiated lessons, group work and child-led learning (what else is there?!) must stand strong – dealing harshly with troublemakers will only decrease student numbers further and make the school appear weak, not unlike Miss Juniper (she'll be alright, though – just needs to toughen up a bit). In any case, someone will throw more money at them: they're too big to fail.

At DA, though, life is simpler. The day begins in silence and carries on as such. Uniform – in house colours, of course – is expected to be worn smartly, misdemeanours are punished consistently and routines are school-wide. The school has bought in one useful piece of technology to save teachers time. This praise and sanctions app allows all manner of behavioural incidents to be very quickly logged and without fuss. Teachers can run their own detentions but are not expected to. There's a dedicated team who deal with behavioural incidents, immediately removing those who disturb learning from classrooms and calling home. At lunch time all children sit together in houses or years, discussing a topic. Children take turns to serve lunch. Instead of spending money on posters about respect, rewards and status badges are purchased. Those awarded talk to their peers in assemblies, gaining respect as they do. As one boy who recently joined from EHS says, "It was tough at first, but I actually enjoy it now. The rules are simple and everyone follows them." And staff feel the same. Teachers want to work here. Nothing's for show, nothing's fake: beneath the cherry is real icing and the fluffiest cake.

Behind location and friendship groups (though in front of Ofsted inspection ratings) parents tend to choose schools with 'discipline/behaviour that promotes effective learning'[35]. Arguably, great behaviour is a cause of every other reason for choosing a school, including Ofsted judgements. But behaviour is also, surely, a huge reason, directly or indirectly, for teachers either leaving a school or the profession entirely. A 2003 study showed that pupil behaviour was the 5th most important reason teachers gave for leaving secondary schools (it was the 8th

---

35 www.nfer.ac.uk/schools/how-do-parents-choose-school-htu.pdf

most important for primaries)[36]. Great behaviour systems lighten workload and lessen stress. They also make schools a more enjoyable place to be. After all, no-one genuinely joined the profession to have a rubbish time, right?

So where to start?

It strikes me that a great behavioural system will have three central tenets:

1. A simple set of rules that places responsibility for behaviour on children. The children need to know this and be reminded at every opportunity.

2. This set of rules as a golden-thread, if you will, at the heart of everything a school is and does. Want politeness? Then insist that children eat at tables with cutlery, for example.

3. A recognition from senior managers that their role is to ensure teachers can teach and children can learn. This means no bureaucracy or blaming teachers for poor behaviour.

Whatever a school chooses for its set of rules (length of tie, phones or none, homework deadlines *etc*) these need to be consistent, predictable and, as much as possible, fair. That means every single teacher must follow the rules as must the children. There are always mavericks in schools, but behaviour mavericks let other teachers and children down. It's simply no good if Mr Fudge lets pass what Miss Juniper immediately squashes, especially if our NQT is following the rules[37]. And here's the thing: following the rules makes a teacher's life easier if those rules are simple, clear and also followed by colleagues. But, if the rules don't support learning, or teacher's decisions aren't supported by managers, then what's the point? It's all in or all out.

Some won't like the word 'rules', I know. There are philosophical arguments about what we mean by obedience and respect, and how we want our children to respond to the world around them. There are those who would argue that imposing rules and adult values on children is somehow fascist, and that we stifle relationships this way. I'd argue the opposite. One of the first things I noticed as a trainee – and this has been borne out in further experience in other challenging schools – is that children like to know where they stand. Having rules, and standing by them, builds relationships better than any "You can call me Dave" type comment. Positive relationships are built on the solid foundations of mutual respect and known boundaries.

---

36 dera.ioe.ac.uk/4759/1/RR430.pdf

37 For some excellent tips on basic classroom routines, see Greg Ashman's 'Top seven classroom management tips' (gregashman.wordpress.com/2016/04/02/my-top-seven-classroom-management-tips/).

And so, these rules must be that golden-thread, that plot-line, around which the school revolves. Want to promote success from hard-work? Have a House or Year system which is at the heart of everything. Like a puppy isn't just for Christmas, so the colouring on the blazers isn't just for Sports Day. Want to engender community spirit? Create student-led groups for all manner of subjects, give them badges and reward their successes outside as well as inside school. Want politeness? Insist on "Good afternoon" from every single student at every single register (you can accept "Good morning" before noon, I guess). Want a quiet and calm atmosphere? The day starts in silence and carries on as such – simple!

None of this is possible, however, without the recognition from senior management that it is children who make choices, for whatever reasons (often out of our control and sometimes as heart-breaking as understandable), and that it is they, not teachers, who must take responsibility for their actions. Anything else is wholly unfair, to the teacher who wants the best for her thirty-two mathematicians, and to the child who must be shown that certain behaviours are unacceptable. And with this recognition must come the acknowledgement that filling out forms, running detentions, telephoning home and attending behavioural meetings, or even the increasingly popular restorative justice meetings, steals precious time that could be better spent doing anything else, like – for instance – running that club, organising that eye-opening trip or, whisper it, planning lessons.

Right, but what can we do?

There's a feeling out there that 'discipline' is a bad word, an action-which-shall-not-be-named: an iron-fisted, *Barad-dûr* relationship slayer, scorching the earth of smiles and laughter. However, this feeling, though doubtless of honourable intention, misunderstands the roles of routine and order. Indeed, relationships with children are built on respect, not engagement and reciprocity. David Didau correctly points out that "Once clear and sensible routines are in place, there is space for positive relationships to form", but only then[38]. Quite so. Relationships must be built on strong foundations, and those foundations are to be found at the very start of the day.

Once a school knows what it wants to promote, it can build a simple set of rules around which all routines are followed. So, let's say a school wants a quiet and calm atmosphere – a valid aim for a place of learning, no? Children, we know, are not always thus, and so we must give them the conditions and

---

38 www.learningspy.co.uk/leadership/behaviour

boundaries in which to succeed: 11 year-olds pumped on two cans of Fiend, or whatever the current fizzy sugarbeast is, are loud. We have to allow them to be quiet.

How about this? The day must begin in silence. Absolute silence. Line them up, in their houses or years, and inspect uniform. Insist on silence. No whispering. No running around. Straight lines, perfect uniform, looking forward, hands out of pockets and blazer sleeves rolled down. Do this for fully five minutes. Each tutor can walk up and down their group, smiling and nodding to all but also sorting out those who are missing their ties and who, for whatever reason, again have forgotten their bags. Any problems are sorted right at the start of the day, everyone is in it together and – most importantly – the bar has been set. Frankly, I'd much rather that bar was way up at "complete silence" than "running around as fast as you possibly can". Wouldn't you? Because if the latter sounds like your school, and you're part of senior management, then you need to sort this. Seriously – it's important.

Anything less than this says to the children, "It's okay – run around and be noisy. We don't mind." And if the school doesn't mind right at the very start of the day then what hope for the next six hours? Teachers cannot expect the best if the best isn't expected and insisted upon every single morning. And as much as a confident teacher might be able to work miracles with even the noisiest group of 16-year-old boys, how much easier would it be for everyone if there was a school norm? Because for every Sgt. Bootstrap there's a couple of Miss Junipers and a few more Mr Fudges.

Anything less than this creates more work for teachers, poorer learning for children and, ultimately, an unhappy and decreasing workforce.

What about the classroom itself? It's very difficult to get children to come back at break or lunch time if they've been five minutes late because "it's only five minutes and why are you so picky have you got OCD or something, 'cause I'm not coming back, I need my lunch and I'm having it, there's nothing you can do." Yeah, okay – that last bit is often true, though.

You have break duty and are meeting some Y11s at lunch, and this in a five-period day (and you should speak to your union about it but haven't the time to even do that): wouldn't it be better if, instead of hiding from the problem of lateness (which, by the way, happens in nearly every school in the world), you marked it down and someone else dealt with it? Yes, management, I'm talking to you again.

It is the student who is late and so their action must be sanctioned. Don't punish the teacher by taking their time away: why not add it all up and send an automated text home? 'Dear Mrs Mushroom, your son Logan was late to [5] lessons today and so will be attending an afterschool detention on [13th January] for [52] minutes.'

There are tons of apps and pieces of software out there which, if supported by managers, could easily reduce workload for everyone. The key thing, though, is not to expect the software to solve the problem of lateness (because it won't, but persistent sanctions might, and if children don't learn – tough). Nor will it reduce workload on its own: it is the subsequent actions of management, made easier by a piece of tech like this, that can make classroom teachers' lives easier.

And what of behavioural policies that allow children to misbehave on a number of occasions, and thus disrupting the learning, before being removed? Well, yes, we want every child to succeed. But we cannot allow the majority of children to fare less well because of a minority's poor choices and subsequent teacher inaction.

Some schools are really pushing the 'no excuses' path at the moment, although they are keen to point out that this is actually a form of love, rather than a renaissance style garrotting of children's characters. Others point to RAG systems where children are given choices with inevitable consequences. And whilst I do feel that allowing children to behave inappropriately on multiple occasions is unacceptable, for them and their irritated peers, whatever policy is in place must be used consistently lest the system fall apart with an inescapable workload increase.

Other decisions that must be made and accepted might include: a year or house system? Or both? And can children gain points, and if so for what rewards? Are academics and music lovers rewarded in the same way that sports enthusiasts are? Is there a 'student hub', or some such, that becomes the new behind-the-bike-shed? What information is shared about behaviour, and does it even need to be shared if everyone has the same expectations? If the time comes to permanently exclude what will the benefit be to other children?

Because whilst alternative provision for the child in question is important, at that moment the more pressing concern must be for his or her peers and the teachers involved. How many forms do teachers have to fill in per behavioural incident? I'd suggest that even one might be going too far. Is behaviour mixed up with SEND? If so, why? What does that say about your school's expectations? Is ADHD an excuse, and if so why? How does that help anyone? Are teachers being honest when they say that they don't really have behavioural issues and, if not, have they ever seen great behaviour?

And finally, and most importantly, are managers being honest about the behaviour in their school?

If a school is worried that all these sanctions might admit to Ofsted that there's a behaviour problem, then oh-my-word what planet are they on? If schools lie about their behaviour problems then they shoot themselves in their clumsy feet. Just be honest: "We have these behavioural issues and this is what we do about it." Because we can't fix society, but we can do everything possible to help those under our care by expecting the best[39]. If we sow chaos and exhaustion then that's what we'll reap. And, actually, that's the harder road to take. It's easier, and more worthwhile for everyone involved, to place the highest vales on behaviour.

"Discipline," as Jo Facer put it, "is the kindest option."[40] The school's responsibility, to both the student and the teacher, is to promote and support great behaviour, and that starts by allowing teachers to teach and children to learn.

Takeaway

Consistency is key to reducing workload: a behaviour policy, including rules, practices, rewards and sanctions, must be applied consistently and actively supported by the leadership team, or the system will fall apart and workload will increase.

Questions

How does your behaviour policy impact on teacher workload? Can you carry out a workload impact assessment?

How bureaucratic are your reporting processes? How can you reduce form filling? Is there technology that you can use?

Do teachers in your school feel that they are individually responsible for poor pupil behaviour, or that they must deal with sanctions (*eg* detention) individually? Does that stop them from reporting problems?

Are your rules clear and simple? Does the whole school know them and follow them? Are the consequences clear and simple? Do all teachers apply them in the same way?

---

39 mrhistoire.com/2016/02/05/behaviour

40 readingallthebooks.com/2016/02/05/discipline

Managing curriculum change while managing workload

Judith Vaughan

Large-scale change and staff workload

When implementing change on a large scale, or introducing an innovative project that reaches to the core of the organisation's fundamental functions, it is important to consider what the impact on staff workload will be.

The school leadership's role is to identify strategies to minimise this where possible and to support staff through any temporary increases where they can't be avoided altogether. In these instances, it will help to map out and share a timeline with clear areas of responsibility so that all parties can see what the expectations of them are.

It is also important that those people who will have to bear workload implications can have an input into the planning as well as the vision and can see the benefits to them and the students in the long term. This is so that, even though there may sometimes be work to do, it is well managed to reduce the stress that might otherwise be associated with it.

This is no less relevant in the area of curriculum design and on-going curriculum development.

Vision

It is important to recognise from the outset of any curriculum design and development that the formal curriculum is only one piece in a larger jigsaw. The values and ethos of the school need to be well understood when considering the timetabled curriculum offer if it is to fit well, reflect accurately the aims of the organisation and therefore be successful.

As school leaders and teachers, our core purpose is to deliver a high quality education for our students. However, there is no definitive set of principles, or rule book, that defines what high quality education is. We must balance the demands of a range of stakeholders with varying ideas of what represents high quality education. Central government dictates statutory curriculum requirements and these are accompanied by accountability systems including performance measures and Ofsted, but these foci are narrow and there is a degree of flexibility beyond what is statutory. Parents and students have their own values and beliefs about what is important and these vary from family to family and even within families. Governors and teachers add further dimensions; the culture of the UK as a whole is diverse and sensitive to media impacts, and the local community within which each school is situated can also influence the direction each school takes.

It is vital to spend some time considering the school's vision, before deciding the shape of the curriculum so that the two work to complement each other rather than differences creating barriers and tensions which in turn cause increased workload for everyone associated with the school.

Supporting staff wellbeing

In addition to school leaders' core purpose of delivering high quality education for students, they are also employers to their staff and have a duty of care for their well-being. In an ideal situation, these two key responsibilities will work in harmony. Valued, happy, engaged and supported staff are likely to also be highly effective in maintaining the core aim of high quality education for students.

In all areas of leadership, I would look for opportunities to consult and collaborate to design sustainable policies with agreed parameters within which staff can exercise a degree of autonomy on an on-going basis. In this way, where there is more partnership and less instruction, where teachers make many of their own decisions about what work they will do to impact on student experience, where personal efficiency is encouraged and nothing is directed to be done without clear purpose in terms of impact on student experience and development, then unnecessary work is minimised.

Curriculum Design

At High Storrs, we consulted widely with staff, students and parents to establish our vision and curriculum principles before working together to develop our innovative curriculum model which was first introduced with Y7 in 2008. Throughout various changes in national educational policy since then we have needed to adjust, refine and tweak our model, but we have regularly revisited our vision and curriculum principles to ensure that each evolution still aligns with the school's ethos and unique character:

We are still an LA school and we have maintained a focus on our specialisms of performing arts, and mathematics and computing. The aim of 'Unlocking Potential' underpins all the work of the school. The five principles that support this vision are:

Key 1: Excellent citizenship

Key 2: High achievement and progress for all

Key 3: Creativity, leadership and accountability

Key 4: A learning school community

Key 5: Making a difference through excellence

Students at High Storrs are entitled to a curriculum which:

- Is broad, balanced and creative with outstanding teaching and learning, and plenty of opportunities for enrichment
- Is inclusive, challenging, experiential and diverse
- Is responsive to individual need through acceleration, differentiation, and alternate pathways when and where appropriate
- Has a wide choice of options to study, but students will study a smaller number at greater depth at any one time
- Has a core element including literacy, numeracy and ICT
- Is relevant to today's society
- Develops Personal, Learning and Thinking Skills
- Values and celebrates diversity and embraces cultural heritage and awareness
- Fosters a sense of identity and community spirit

We have a two-year Key Stage 3, then students take a series of one year courses within differentiated pathways through their three-year Key Stage 4. This structure is in part to ensure maximum flexibility for students in choosing their Key Stage 4 courses.

Originally, we had to consider carefully the structure of this curriculum to ensure we were delivering the statutory curriculum, appropriate Key Stage 3 foundation for further study at Key Stage 4 and beyond as well as making sure student experience didn't feel 'rushed' at any point. We felt there was overlap between many of our Key Stage 3 courses in terms of skills and some content.

We worked to align subjects so that we made the most of these overlaps in terms of available curriculum time. We tried to have a more collaborative approach between subjects and introduced faculties as a way of grouping subjects to facilitate this collaboration. Teaching staff were involved at the design stage and heavily invested in the model and their part within it. Consequently, they have seen the benefits now of the work they put in at the outset in terms of breadth of student choice on offer, including the inclusion of minority subjects which might otherwise have vanished from the curriculum.

In Key Stage 4 (see figure 1), students' individual curriculum plans can be built within a very flexible framework. The key features of the structure that support this ideal are as follows:

· Students study English, Maths and Science for the full three years. They take the examinations for these courses at the end of year 11.

· In year 8 students select their options courses. They have two options for each year, giving them six options in total.

· The options process, though potentially complex to understand is well designed to minimise workload for staff and stress for students – providing students and their parents with the information, support and time that they need to make the right choices.

· Each of the options courses is delivered within a year and taught for five hours per week.

· As well as GCSE (and equivalent) courses, students can take enrichment and preliminary courses, which allow students to explore a wider range of subjects than would traditionally be on offer.

· For some subjects, for example history, geography, languages, and music students take a preliminary course to ensure that they are fully prepared for the GCSE.

· Options courses are taught in mixed year groups, including students from years 9, 10 and 11. This allows for a wide range of subjects to achieve sufficient student numbers to run courses which helps to keep the curriculum broad and balanced, but also affordable.

Figure 1 shows the structure of the 25 hour week across each KS4 year. The Options blocks in hours 16 – 25 represent the mixed Y9-11 classes where students can map out a mixture of five hour exam course options, two or three hour pre-GCSE options and one hour, non-examined enrichment course options in each year:

	1	2	3	4	5	6	7	8	9	10	11	12	13	14	15	16	17	18	19	20	21	22	23	24	25
Y9	Maths				PSE	English				PE		Science				EX	EY	EZ			AX		AY		AZ

	1	2	3	4	5	6	7	8	9	10	11	12	13	14	15	16	17	18	19	20	21	22	23	24	25
Y10	Maths				PSE	English				PE		Science				EX	EY	EZ			AX		AY		AZ

	1	2	3	4	5	6	7	8	9	10	11	12	13	14	15	16	17	18	19	20	21	22	23	24	25
Y11	Maths				PSE	English				PE		Science				EX	EY	EZ			AX		AY		AZ

Figure 1

Through careful planning of the options process and timetable, students are offered a broad range of subjects to study. Students are well supported in the process of choosing their options and value both the wide range of courses on offer and the ability to spread their GCSEs out over three years. The running of the Y8 Options process each year is a significant undertaking and the reviews in Y9 and Y10 also take time and energy.

All staff receive refresher training every year just before the start of the programme, which spreads the load of supporting students widely amongst the whole staff and reduces possible anxiety for tutors in particular. There is a co-ordinated range of activities for students designed to strengthen their understanding, so that they bring their own expertise to the process, minimising pressure on teachers and indeed parents.

Teachers value the intensive, focused time they get with each Key Stage 4 exam class – fewer classes, but more time with each makes planning and assessment more efficient. Teachers have had to refine their planning for differentiation for classes with wider age ranges than traditionally taught, and we have put time and resources into training and development in this area. This is expertise staff have been able to use in all their teaching across the key stages.

Overall, the elements that have brought increased workload temporarily or where energies have needed to be re-distributed, have been accepted by teachers because they understand and value the wider benefits of the model for them and for students.

Making time to review

As a result of recent national changes in curriculum, assessment and accountability policies we have been reviewing and modifying our practice to create a five- year curriculum and assessment plan from year 7 to GCSE, in which students will experience one continuous learning journey.

Once again this work has engaged directly with teachers; this time the drive has come via the Teaching and Learning Strategy Group which includes all subject leaders. Critically, we have made every effort to be ahead of national changes and allow plenty of lead in time for staff to prepare. There is never enough time, but we have been committed to ensuring that the time we do have through INSET and meeting time is used well. Much of this time has been given over to subject teams to engage in thinking and planning once the key whole school principles and over-arching strategy have been agreed.

At High Storrs, we try not to constrain the autonomy and creativity of teachers by insisting on overly prescriptive parameters. Instead, we work to ensure we have a shared understanding of the vision for any development across the whole staff before smaller teams embark on building their own ideas. In this way, subject teams and individual teachers can focus on what will work best for their subject and for them as an individual in impacting on student progress, without creating unnecessary workload trying to make this fit within a rigid prescribed structure.

Before making any changes to our Key Stage 3 curriculum offer, staff spent time analysing the new national curriculum and comparing it to what they already taught. Subject teams then decided how to adapt their existing schemes of work to meet the requirements of the new national curriculum as well as ensuring firm foundations for GCSE and the inclusion of desirable enrichment content. Due to the flexibility of the existing curriculum, the underlying structure did not need to be changed.

We used the national curriculum and assessment changes to thoroughly review our entire curriculum offer. Each subject team reviewed their curriculum plans to create an overview that had a logical journey from year 7 to year 11. With the removal of levels, we designed and introduced our own Assessment and Progression Criteria Frameworks which map out the core skills, knowledge and understanding required for progress in each subject to span years 7-11. These are aligned to adapted 1-9 grades that are being introduced with the new GCSEs.

Ensuring that students have fully grasped the essential content of each subject drives the new assessment system. This is a key element towards our intention that our curriculum is one continuous learning journey. We have been working on the development of the new system for some time, and we are realistic about the need to review and refine it following implementation and as our understanding of new qualifications deepens.

Developing the new system has been a slow and carefully planned process.

Time, effective communication and support are essential ingredients of successful curriculum and assessment change. Staff need to feel involved, supported and also have the time to plan properly. As a leadership team, we have focused on being very clear in our communication, ensuring that teaching staff have been aware of key developments in their subject areas and given over much inset time to planning for these changes.

The lead in time for the new assessment system has been almost two years, with key points flagged on the timeline for particular elements to be completed at least in draft form. This has enabled subject teams to review schemes of work and devise the new Assessment and Progression Criteria Frameworks with sufficient time and space to review and discuss them fully.

We have prioritised which aspects of the school's response to policy change are fixed (the new 1-9 assessment system) and which are flexible (the format of schemes of work) and offered one to one support to each subject leader. Subject leaders have worked in collaboration with their team, each other and other subject leaders across the city to implement change. Subject teams work well together to ensure that not only does every teacher have a voice, but also to ensure that everyone understands and is on board with the new developments.

The teaching staff at High Storrs are very aware that doing things thoroughly the first time will make reviewing them the second time much easier.

Wider communication

It is really important to bring not only staff, but also governors, parents and students on the change journey with you. If the expectations of all stakeholders are considered and well managed, then work generated from responding to queries and alleviating alarm can be minimised.

At High Storrs, our curriculum model is unusual and although we are not the only school in the country with a three-year Key Stage 4, or to deliver some one-year GCSEs, the detail of our model is unique. This means we have needed to give a lot of thought to how we communicate it to parents and students. Students and parents are given a lot of support throughout the options process and we've also taken time to explain about changes to assessment in the school.

Communication with parents is very strong at High Storrs, and parents respond positively to the frank and honest presentations that we provide. Senior leaders regularly discuss with governors the work that is going on in school around curriculum and assessment (see Emma Knights' chapter for more on how governors can support school leaders). This includes emerging ideas, progress reports about how things are developing and sharing evaluative work, including staff, student and parent voice reflections, as well as scrutiny of results analysis that helps support reflections on the success of models used in the school.

When making their options choices, students have support from their form tutor, class teachers, PSHCEE teacher, members of SLT and their parents – everyone in the school understands the structure and can offer advice and guidance. Information is presented clearly and students are encouraged to take the lead in mapping out their choices. Taster lessons and information evenings help students and parents to fully understand the options on offer.

Consequently, the students have a strong understanding of how the curriculum works and how to get the most out of it. They value the support that they are given and enjoy the curriculum that they choose.

We talk to a sample of Y8 students at the end of the options process in small focus groups to evaluate how the process has gone for them. We have also used questionnaires with Y11 students to check their levels of satisfaction with the curriculum model they've been through. There is always lots of positive feedback, but we also find things that need attention and these feed into the on-going evolution of the whole model. Some of the adjustments we have made over the years since implementation have been due to national education policy change, others have been around reflections on results analysis, but students' input has also been a determining factor in any changes we've made.

> What the students say about the High Storrs Curriculum:
> - High Storrs students are very proud of their curriculum.
> - They enjoy the flexibility it offers them in designing their own bespoke pathways.
> - They feel supported by the vertical tutor system, mixed year group options classes and the school staff.
> - They welcome the fact that they can spread their GCSEs out over three years.
> - They are grateful to their teachers for understanding their individual interests and providing opportunities inside and outside of the classroom.
> - They think that the new assessment system will work well once they have got used to it.

Reflecting on the vision

It is well worth taking time to regularly reflect on the school's work, including specific initiatives in the context of the school's vision. At High Storrs, the underpinning principle to the school's vision is 'unlocking potential'. In this context, we can check the strength of our curriculum and the way we have worked with the whole school community to evolve it:

- We responded to curriculum changes in a way that enabled us to hold on to our performing arts specialism which is fundamental to the school's ethos. Students' confidence is built through this specialism and they are able to sustain their involvement both within and beyond the formal curriculum. This is part of how we unlock student potential, not only through highly successful exam outcomes in these areas of the curriculum, but also through development of the whole student – it provides opportunities for creativity, excellence, school community and citizenship.
- Senior leaders have worked hard to keep track of national policy announcements, and communicate what this means to governors, staff, students and parents so that the whole school community has time to respond creatively, leading to high achievement and progress for all.
- Ensuring that teachers have had time to think, reflect and plan for the assessment and curriculum changes means their potential for excellence is not stifled. They have had space for their own learning in a way that contributes to the whole school community.
- Change has not been rushed, and much of the success of the curriculum is down to the strong preparation process that we, as senior leaders, have designed.
- Students have a strong sense of their own learning journey, which begins at transition and ends in highly successful GCSE results.

Key lessons in planning curriculum change

- Keeping track of national policy announcements is vital.
- Have the confidence to adapt what already works well within the school curriculum, rather than starting from scratch.
- When big change is planned – like the new assessment system – allow plenty of planning and thinking time for staff and expect to continue working on it after initial implementations.
- Create a culture in which teams work together to consolidate subject

knowledge and feel able to have frank discussions about the future of the curriculum.

- Be honest with parents and students even if sometimes you have to highlight the things that aren't clear yet.
- Don't let your school curriculum be dominated by the whims of a secretary of state, remember your strengths and continue to play to them.
- Put the students first and stay true to your school values and ethos.

Take-away

Sustainable change takes time. Good communication is key, along with using the time you have – in meetings and INSET days – wisely.

Key lessons in managing workload

- Are your systems sustainable? Everything has to be affordable and manageable. Don't design something so radical that the drive from leadership has to be constant.
- Are your monitoring systems both sufficient to hold staff to account, and also manageable? Demands should not result in burnout for teachers or leaders.
- Is everyone in the school community encouraged to work in a streamlined and efficient way? Look for minimum input for maximum output. Don't do anything for the sake of it, everything needs a clear purpose linked to the school vision for student experience and outcomes.
- Do your teachers and teams have autonomy? Staff need to have maximum involvement and ownership. No-one wants to work excessively to up-hold someone else's ideal, but goodwill stretches further when the vision is truly shared. Trust your staff, they are professionals. Don't try and put square pegs in round holes.
- How can you think creatively to find time to plan collaboratively and develop ideas at all levels to achieve trust and autonomy?

Making time for CPD

Heath Monk

A brief modern history of workload

Excessive teacher workload is not a new phenomenon. My first role, on leaving the classroom for the Department for Education back in 2001, was in the 'Reducing Bureaucracy' team. Our task was to find ways to cut the amount of paperwork that fell to schools and teachers, enabling them to focus on what mattered most – teaching.

We would wage war on the myriad of forms and returns emanating from the Department, subjecting policy teams to a Star Chamber in which they had to justify why they needed to collect data from schools. In those days, however, the Standards Fund drove policy, with small pots of money linked to reporting requirements. Ministerial desire usually overcame official reluctance – and the Star Chamber did little more than collect some low-hanging fruit.

Besides, bureaucracy wasn't really the core of the problem. What the Department didn't (and doesn't) seem to understand was that the act of teaching groups of children (and the preparation and assessment that inevitably goes along with it) takes up the majority of a teacher's time.

In 2002, following an extensive piece of research into the drivers of teacher workload undertaken by PwC, the Department published 'Time for Standards' which sought to address three areas that seemed to offer some practical ways forward: administrative tasks, cover and guaranteed time during the school day for planning, preparation and assessment (PPA).

These recommendations were incorporated in the National Agreement on Workforce Reform, signed in January 2003 with the headteacher, teacher and support staff unions (with the exception of the NUT). Together, and supported by the National Remodelling Team, we undertook a three year change programme to help schools implement the contractual changes set out in the National Agreement.

For a while, there were some signs of success. Average working hours (evidenced by the STRB-led diary surveys) edged down, with particular reduction in time spent on administration. Schools employed scores of teaching assistants to support their teaching staff (although they may have done better to employ teacher assistants instead, tasked with supporting the teacher, rather than working directly with small groups of children).

However, looking back, I now realise that we were little more than modern-day King Cnuts – engaged in a battle against a tide that simply would not be turned.

In 2010, the Coalition decided that the contractual changes made by the National Agreement were a form of micro-management (in the days where autonomy was still a big ideal) and scrapped them. The last vestiges of three years of work were washed away – and the tide of teacher workload rose inexorably higher.

At least contractual change was a valiant attempt to reduce workload. The recent Workload Challenge, which took over a year from inception to any sign of activity, contained a series of recommendations that were well-meaning, but ultimately meaningless. And the appeal to the Department for Education not to introduce major changes in-year lasted for only a matter of weeks before the recent tumultuous series of policy pronouncements, U-turns and gaffes.

In fact, I believe that we are at a point where workload represents a significant threat to teacher supply and, therefore, the quality of education offered to young people. In a recent survey conducted by The Key[41], 84% of school leaders said that they had struggled with managing workload over the past year. 57% report that workload has had a detrimental effect on their mental health. And workload is a major factor in the decision taken by a growing number of teachers to leave the profession.

I offer this brief history lesson as context for the challenge faced in ensuring that teachers have access to high-quality CPD and the appetite and time to take it up. Even when recruitment to the profession was buoyant, it would have taken a generation to renew the stock of teachers – we have always been in the position where 'loving the ones you're with' (CPD) is more important than new blood (ITT). Now, when NCTL has consistently missed its teacher training targets, retention and the development of the hard-pressed and demoralised workforce is simply essential.

So how, when teachers are drowning under the pressures placed upon them by increasingly demanding external expectations, can CPD find a productive space?

To answer that question, we must first look at the difference between real and perceived workload.

---

41 www.joomag.com/magazine/state-of-education-survey-report-2016/0604114001462451154?short

What motivates?

I do not mean, in any way, to suggest that the problem of excessive workload is not real. Instead, what was striking from the PwC research was the extent to which the number of hours worked and the 'workload' felt as a result of those hours are two very different things, with much less correlation than might be imagined.

In fact, the perception of excessive workload is caused by two main factors: the extent to which work is imposed on a teacher and the extent to which it is seen by that teacher to be lacking in intrinsic value.

Daniel Pink's 'Drive'[42] suggests that deep motivation is made up of three elements: mastery, autonomy and purpose. Imposed, pointless work goes against the latter two of those elements. When we are not motivated, every minute seems like an hour. Activities are painful and resented – we imagine how much better this time could be spent, if only...

In contrast, there are times when we feel a sense of 'flow' in our work, as described by Mihály Csíkszentmihályi[43]. What we are doing is deeply engrossing – time seems to race by and we wish we had more of it to devote to the activity in which we're engaged.

The difference cannot be measured in time.

By way of example, the National Agreement had mandated that teachers should no longer put up classroom displays. It was felt that this was a time-consuming task that could be undertaken by someone else. However, I met many teachers who told me that they loved putting up displays – it sent a powerful signal to their classes about the value in which their work was held and it was an intrinsically satisfying experience. They were determined to carry on, even if it meant coming in at weekends.

The same was rarely true for data entry.

In part, that is because great displays also engage the third of Daniel Pink's drivers: mastery. There is great satisfaction in learning to be really, really good at something; in developing genuine expertise. At School 21 in Stratford, the curriculum is based around the creation of 'beautiful work'; its values include craftsmanship.

---

42 Pink D H (2009) Drive, the surprising truth about what motivates us New York: Riverhead Books (Penguin)

43 See for example Csíkszentmihályi M (1992) Flow: the psychology of happiness USA: Harper and Row

Compliance or craftsmanship?

However, for many teachers (and students), school has become more about compliance than craftsmanship. School policies on lesson planning and marking are imposed at a whim (on the basis of something someone overheard about the new Ofsted framework at a conference), without considering the cost in terms of motivation. What had been a positive experience (how best can I introduce this concept to my class?) quickly becomes a pointless chore (have I filled in the proforma?). Consider the difference between trying to make the perfect chocolate cake for a birthday party and cooking family dinner for the fifth day in a row.

Of course, there is a need for consistency in schools. Behaviour policy, for example, is an area where I believe that schools need to be clear, consistent and rigorous (see the chapter by Toby French). However, it must be understood that every attempt to introduce more consistency comes with a significant risk of reducing motivation and increasing perceived workload.

Worse than that, too much of what is currently designated as CPD actually consists of nothing more than compliance training, whether that is imposed at national, school or department level. Learning about a new assessment measure, exam specification or appraisal process is training, not development – and yet in many schools the vast majority of CPD time (usually in the form of the dreaded INSET days) is spent on such activities.

I would love to think that a future Secretary of State will come to the realisation that the success of schools depends more on the motivation and quality of the staff that work in them than any policy change made by central Government (see Mary Bousted's chapter for more on government policy). However, I am not hopeful on that score – at the moment, it seems that almost every announcement made by Ministers is aimed at centralising power within the DfE on the basis that it alone knows best how to improve educational standards.

If there is to be no respite at national level, the onus falls on school leaders (and increasingly those that lead MATs) to ensure that they seek to reduce, not increase, the level of compliance required in their organisations. Leaders need to be judicious and discerning when mandating a particular practice within their schools – and where compliance is absolutely necessary, they should be clear about its purpose; understand the implications on workload (will this be more efficient and if not, what else will we stop doing?); and give individuals as much freedom as possible in the 'how' of a given task.

By doing this, leaders can provide the space for teachers to engage in meaningful professional development, driven by a desire for mastery, autonomy and purpose. Because, whatever the right-wing press might say, the vast majority of teachers are dedicated professionals who want to do a good job. No-one comes into teaching for the money. However, the commitment to making a difference to the lives of children is too often dulled by endless top-down change, rather than sharpened by new discovery.

What sort of CPD should we make (more) time for?

That is not to say that CPD should be left to chance. There should be an expectation that every teacher seeks to improve the quality of their practice every year. The issue is whether that improvement is achieved through compliance with another set of new procedures or through professional dialogue, practice, feedback and reflection.

The job of school leaders becomes, then, to create a culture where genuine development can take place. There are several elements to this:

- Access to genuine expertise: while much development can take place among peers within the school, there remains a place for external expertise, whether in the form of speakers, school visits or access to research studies. Inputs should be based on evidence (rather than showmanship) and presented as stimuli for discussion and practice (rather than the start of a new prescriptive practice). Ensuring a regular diet of such ideas is, I would argue, motivating for teachers – the growing popularity of #TeachMeets would certainly seem to endorse this view.

- Freedom to take risks: development is born out of failure. Anyone who has learned a musical instrument or played a sport has experienced the challenge of learning new and more complex techniques – you inevitably get worse before you get better. However, if I am solely judged on my performance today, I am much more likely to stay within my comfort zone and stagnate, than take a risk and grow.

- Feedback: feedback is a gift. Of course, to be effective, it must be given in the spirit of a gift – that is with a genuine desire to help the receiver and at a time when it is likely to be well-received. In such circumstances (and in a culture where it is not just safe to take risks, but doing so is positively encouraged), it is amazing how direct and powerful feedback can be, freed from the dreadful euphemisms of the 'performance management' conversation.

- Time for reflection: there must be opportunities for teachers to reflect on their learning and their goals. Coaching can play a part in this – and I have visited several schools that have employed teacher coaches extensively

— as it provides a space focused on discussion led by the teacher, not the coach. Peer groups can also be a powerful way of encouraging reflection.

However, the fundamental underpinning of a culture where CPD can thrive is trust.

The current model of accountability has, at its heart, the premise that, unless I check up on everything that you do, you will seek to get away with as much as possible. On that basis, improvement in results is purely down to the pressure of league tables, Ofsted and constant monitoring. The job of the manager is to catch you doing something wrong; to shift the goalposts regularly to avoid complacency; and to be absolutely unforgiving in the castigation of wrong-doers *'pour encourager les autres'*.

This is not true accountability at all! How can I be held to account for my choices and actions if everything that I am expected to do has been prescribed for me in advance?

A culture based on trust does exactly the opposite. It says that you are a professional, motivated to do the best for your students. My role is to provide you with the tools and information to do that job as effectively as possible and with as much freedom as I can allow, given the constraints necessary within the system. You will be expected to account for yourself, but when something goes wrong, we will try to understand what caused the issue, rather than simply assign blame.

John Blakey's *The Trusted Executive*[44] provides an accessible and powerful toolkit for creating trust within an organisation. He places the development of trust in the wider context of increased transparency, globalisation and public expectations, especially from a millennial generation raised on social media. The traditional model of success, built on competence and authority, has broken down, as increased access to information and better choices means that consumers and employees are more demanding. Instead, great leadership is built on three pillars: ability, integrity and benevolence.

I am not suggesting that schools should become a free-for-all. In a democratic society, it is right that Government should oversee the school system and demand higher standards, especially for the most disadvantaged. In a successful school, there are times when the need for consistency outweighs the benefits of professional autonomy. There will always be a certain amount of paperwork and compliance-based training.

However, if we want to see genuine CPD – which stands, after all, for continuing

44 johnblakey.co.uk

professional development – we need to reduce the amount of compliance to a minimum, in order to create time and space for lasting development to happen within a culture of trust.

Creating this culture may not reduce teachers' hours (in fact, I suspect that teachers will end up working for as many, if not more, hours than they do now), but it will have huge impact on their perceived workload, their job satisfaction and, most importantly, the quality of education for the nation's children.

Takeaway

Work becomes workload when it is seen to be pointless and when it is imposed.

Genuine development takes place through professional dialogue, practice, feedback and reflection: to make time, you need to remove unnecessary activity and reduce compliance training to a bare minimum.

Questions

What is the balance of compliance and craftsmanship in your own practice? In your school? In the CPD you undertake?

Is this view of the balance commonly held by your colleagues? Are you happy with it?

What motivates you and gets you into a state of 'flow'? What CPD would help you to develop or share your skills in these areas?

Can you audit your school's CPD against the five elements identified in this chapter?

- · Access to genuine expertise
- · Freedom to take risks
- · Feedback
- · Time for reflection
- · Trust

A quick guide to marking

(adapted from ATL's workload campaign pages)

What's the problem?

It takes too long

It's too complex, or it's done too frequently

It's not done to benefit pupils, but so that others can see

'Basically, you never sleep or you are never up to date with marking.'

Should marking be done at all?

Marking pupils' work can be an important part of assessment. Amongst other things, it enables a teacher to

- evaluate whether a pupil has understood/learnt what has been taught;
- reflect on whether they need to provide additional/different support for a pupil;
- reflect on whether they need to address a topic differently for groups or classes
- evaluate whether a pupil is making progress with skills, knowledge, understanding
- provide feedback to a pupil to enable them to make progress
- provide a score or grade for summative purposes.

Marking isn't the only way of doing these things, but it is a very visible mechanism, and everyone likes to see the teacher's red pen (or perhaps the pink, green or purple pen) as evidence that something has been happening.

However, as Paul Black and Dylan Wiliam said back in 1998 in *Inside the Black Box*[45], feedback is too often used for managerial purposes at the expense of learning functions; collection of marks is given greater priority than analysis of work to discern pupils' learning needs.

What does good practice look like?

Evidence on marking is limited. The Education Endowment Fund (EEF) review in

---

45 www.spd.dcu.ie/site/teaching_today/documents/raisingstandardsthrough classroomassessment.pdf

April 2016[46] points to the fact that none of their projects have looked specifically at marking, and EEF has earmarked £2m to fund new trials.

Evidence on feedback is clear. The EEF Toolkit[47] says it should be specific, accurate and clear; it should encourage further effort, and be given sparingly so that it is meaningful; it should be about complex or challenging tasks or goals; and it can come from peers as well as adults.

Black and Wiliam demonstrate that pupil self-assessment is a vital part of assessment for learning, and that it is successful when pupils have a sufficiently clear view of the targets their learning is meant to attain. Also see the EPPi systematic review of self- and peer-assessment in secondary schools (2008)[48]

Peer assessment and marking doesn't just happen. It is most effective when pupils are supported to understand the objectives they are trying to meet, and given frameworks for providing constructive feedback. See NFER's guidance on assessment[49] for more information.

How can you make marking more manageable?

Use the DfE Workload working group suggestions, and see more information on those in the chapters from Nansi Ellis and Mary Myatt.

Think about whether any of these ideas could help reduce your workload

- more peer and self-assessment
- sparing use of more detailed marking and written feedback appropriate to children's age and stage
- shared/longer blocks of protected non-teaching time for assessment and marking.

Have realistic expectations

- Four hours marking a night is not realistic. Teachers and senior leaders need conversations about how much time they should expect to spend marking each week.

---

46 Elliott V et al (2016) A marked improvement: a review of the evidence on written marking EEF/ University of Oxford educationendowmentfoundation.org.uk/public/files/Publications/ EEF_Marking_Review_April_2016.pdf

47 educationendowmentfoundation.org.uk/toolkit/toolkit-a-z/feedback/

48 eppi.ioe.ac.uk/cms/Default.aspx?tabid=2415

49 www.nfer.ac.uk/schools/getting-to-grips-with-assessment/getting-to-grips-with-assessment-4.pdf

- Marking every piece of work is not realistic. Agreements are needed about which pieces of work should be marked, and which should NOT be marked.
- It is not realistic to expect every subject and every age group to be marked in the same way. Subject and phase leaders should consider what will have the most impact on pupils' learning.

Think about how best to give feedback to pupils

- Pupils respond to feedback better if there is less but better feedback.
- Feedback is effective when it is immediate, when pupils can respond and ask questions, and when it is given at key points in children's learning – when it will directly affect their next piece of work.
- We need to be able to say 'well done' and identify pupils' strengths without always having to tell them how to do better.

Find different ways of assessing pupils' learning

- Formative assessment (assessment for learning) is a vital part of teaching and should not be seen as an 'add on'. It takes time, and senior leaders will need to think about how to free up time for teachers to assess collaboratively and to improve their skills.
- Teachers need opportunities to develop pupils' self- and peer-assessment skills

Think about how to evidence effective feedback

- Senior leaders need to quality assure teachers' assessment, to support those who need it, and to be confident that assessment is happening across the school. But this doesn't mean checking that books have been marked and verbal feedback is written down. Nor does it mean pupils must respond in writing to written feedback.
- Class teachers and pupils should be aware of their strengths and areas of development. Senior leaders could have conversations about them. They don't need to be written down.
- Clear evidence of pupil progress in their work, for example through drafting stages, should be evidence of effective assessment and feedback.

How to cut your workload by reducing your marking load

- Don't mark everything. Can you agree a clear plan for what should be marked, and importantly what should NOT be marked? Which aspects of marking will have the most impact on pupils' learning?

- Don't spend four hours a night marking. Can you agree how much time you should spend marking and then work out how to use that time? For example, if your senior leadership team agree that three hours marking a week is reasonable (as in Finland, according to TALIS), and it takes an hour to mark a set of books, which three sets will you mark, and how will you assess other aspects of work?
- Marking isn't the only way of assessing pupils' learning. Can you develop a toolkit of different ways of assessing? Which ones are most effective at raising pupils' attainment, improving pupil outcomes or deepening pupils' learning?

Questions to discuss with colleagues/senior leadership

- Which aspects of marking, if any, have the most positive impact?
- What is the impact of the current level of marking on teachers' workload and wellbeing?
- How should we plan the assessment, marking and feedback we will undertake so that marking is useful for pupils and teachers?
- How does/will our marking help us to celebrate the achievements of pupils?
- Does our marking/assessment policy reflect the values and ethos of the school?
- How can we improve the quality of marking, and particularly the quality of feedback, without increasing the overall workload?
- How will we explain to parents when and how we mark, so that they understand why their child's work doesn't have teacher comments, ticks or stamps on every page?
- How and when will we develop children's self- and peer-assessment skills?
- When and how (and how often) will we review children's self- and peer-assessment so that we can reflect on their skills and their work in order to improve our teaching?
- How and when can we deepen our understanding of formative assessment (assessment for learning), and in particular on what kinds of feedback are most useful for pupils' learning?
- How and when can we work collaboratively on assessment?
- If we are required to set and mark tests, what work shall we not mark in order to make time for test marking?
- If you can stop marking one set of books each week (which could give you 90 minutes), what will you do with that time?

Handling stress in education

Julian Stanley

Teaching today is a juggling act of grand proportions with the need to balance the increased responsibilities for testing and assessment with growing class sizes and a reduction in administrative and support staff[50]. So it's no wonder that teachers are experiencing high levels of work place strain with workload being predominantly to blame.

But it doesn't have to be this way. At the Education Support Partnership, we help thousands of those working in all sectors of education to be at their best, through our counselling, support and professional development. As such we know that, with the right wellbeing programmes, management support and development structures in place, education can still be one of the most rewarding, unique and exciting sectors around.

Ultimately though, the challenges the sector is currently experiencing need careful management and individual tenacity to ensure that one can remain healthy and happy at work.

This chapter provides a range of constructive tips and advice to individuals and people managers across the education sector in order to help ensure working life is as stress free and rewarding as possible.

What is stress?

According to the Health and Safety Executive, the definition of workplace stress is as follows:

> 'Stress is the reaction people have to excessive pressures or other types of demand placed on them.[51]'

By this, we mean an adverse reaction to the demands of the environment. We want to distinguish between pressures or challenges, which can be stimulating, and stress, which is the reaction to too much pressure.

In other words, people experience stress as they adjust to a continually changing environment. Stress has physical and emotional effects, and the associated pressure can create both positive and negative feelings.

---

50 www.theguardian.com/education/2016/apr/05/school-deprivation-funding-changes-education-budget

51 www.hse.gov.uk/stress/furtheradvice/whatisstress.htm

Positive pressure can energise you and help you reach your peak performance. Too much pressure can turn into stress. Prolonged exposure to stress can be harmful to your physical and mental wellbeing so one of the first steps to managing stress is to understand what the causes are.

Sources of Stress

There are a wide range of sources of stress. These include daily hassles, major life events, home and work factors. Try to consider, what are the things in your life that might cause you stress?

Home stress factors can include	Work stress factors can include
• relationships • money problems • children • sickness • housework	• Overload • Relationships • Pace of change • Deadlines • Unrealistic workloads or demands

Stress Signs

As a first step, it's helpful to know your stress signs and recognise the ways that you react to stress. Which of the following do you experience?

- Muscle tension
- Headaches
- Indigestion
- Dry mouth
- Diarrhoea or constipation
- Anxiety/excessive worry
- Difficulty concentrating
- Forgetfulness
- Irritability
- Depression
- Boredom
- Apathy
- Change in sleep patterns
- Withdrawal
- Accident proneness
- Reduced sex drive
- Increase in use of drugs, smoking or alcohol
- Tearfulness

Some of these signs may have causes other than stress. Check with your doctor if symptoms persist.

Building Stress Prevention

The following may help to relieve symptoms of stress:

- Exercising three to four times a week to reduce muscle tension
- Minimising intake of sugar, caffeine and other artificial stimulants
- Getting enough rest

- Practising at least one relaxation exercise
- Getting up 15 minutes earlier in the morning (making morning mishaps less stressful)
- Listening to music
- Making time for fun
- Unplugging your phone

Stress Strategies

In order to get stress under control you need to understand where it comes from, what you can do about it and how. The points below are designed to help you in that process.

> Step 1: Awareness – Ask yourself these questions:
> - What are the sources of stress in my life?
> - What are my emotional and physical reactions to them?
> - What are my strengths in dealing with stress? (*eg* "I delegate well".)
> - What are my limitations in dealing with stress? (*eg* "I sometimes have difficulty saying no to work requests".)

> Step 2: Plan – Develop a plan of action by asking yourself these questions:
> - What sources of stress can I eliminate or avoid?
> - What sources of stress are changeable?
> - What one change could I start with that would make the most difference in my life?
> - Who can I enlist in helping or supporting me with this change?
> - How can I include taking care of myself in my plan?

> Step 3: Action
> Choose one new strategy to add to or change about your current approach to dealing with stress. Importantly remember to deal with the sources of stress that you can change (create a plan to eliminate, reduce or avoid these sources).

Eleven practical tips for dealing with stress

Having identified the cause of your stress, here are some suggestions of how to address it;

1. Put your body in motion

Physical activity is one of the most effective ways of keeping stress away, by clearing your head and lifting your spirits. Physical activity also increases endorphin levels – the 'feel-good' chemicals that leave you with a naturally happy feeling. So whether you like full-fledged games of football, tennis or roller hockey, or you prefer walks with family and friends, it's important to get up, get out and get moving!

2. Fuel up

If your body was a car, you wouldn't go for a long drive without filling up on petrol first. Likewise, begin each day by eating breakfast to give you the energy you need to tackle the day. Eating regular meals (this means no skipping dinner) and taking time to enjoy them (eating in the car doesn't count) will make you feel better too. Make sure to fuel up with fruits, vegetables, proteins (peanut butter, a chicken sandwich or a tuna salad) and grains (wheat bread, pasta or some crackers) – these will give you the slow-release energy you need to make it through those hectic days. Don't be fooled by the jolt of energy you get from fizzy drinks and sugary snacks – this only lasts a short time, and once it wears off, you may feel sluggish and more tired than usual. For that extra boost grab a banana, some string cheese or a granola bar.

3. LOL (Laugh Out Loud)

Did you know that it takes 15 facial muscles to laugh? Lots of laughing can make you feel good – and that good feeling can stay with you even after the laughter stops. Head off stress with regular doses of laughter by watching a funny movie or cartoons, reading a joke book or even make up your own riddles – laughter can make you feel like a new person! Everyone has those days when they do something really silly or stupid – instead of getting upset with yourself, laugh out loud! No one's perfect!

4. Have fun with friends

Being with people you like is always a good way to ditch your stress. Get a group together to go to the cinema, do some exercise, listen to music or play a board game – or just hang out and talk.

5. Talk to someone you trust

Instead of keeping your feelings bottled up inside, talk to someone you trust or respect about what's bothering you. It could be a friend, a parent, someone in your family, someone from your religious or spiritual community, or a supervisor or teacher. Talking about your problems and seeing them from a different view might help you figure out ways to deal with them. Just remember, you don't have to go at it alone!

6. Take time to relax

Practice relaxation techniques. Pick a comfy spot to sit and read, daydream or even take a snooze. Listen to your favourite music. Work on a relaxing project like putting together a puzzle or making jewellery. Stress can sometimes make you feel like a tight rubber band – stretched to the limit. If this happens, take a few deep breaths to help yourself unwind. If you're in the middle of an impossible problem, take a break! Finding time to relax after (and sometimes during) a hectic day or week can make all the difference.

7. Take a break

Fatigue is stress's best friend. When you're over-tired, a problem may seem much bigger than it actually is. You may have a hard time doing a work assignment that usually seems easy, you may not do your best in sports or any physical activity, or you may have an argument with your friends or partner over something really stupid. Sleep is a big deal!

8. Keep a journal

Identifying what you do well (and not so well) when managing your stress can really help. If you're having one of those crazy days when nothing goes right, it's a good idea to write things down in a journal to get it off your chest – how you feel, what's going on in your life and things you'd like to accomplish. You could even write down what you do when you're faced with a stressful situation, and then look back and think about how you handled it later. Find a quiet spot, grab a notebook and pen, and start writing!

9. Perfect planning prevents poor performance

Do you have too much to do, but not enough time? Are you feeling overwhelmed or forgetful at work? Being unprepared for work or other activities can make for a very stressful day. Getting everything done can be a challenge, but being organised and planning in advance can help.

10. Lend a hand

Get involved in an activity that helps others. It's almost impossible to feel stressed out when you're helping someone else. It's also a great way to find out about yourself and the special talents you never knew you had. Signing up for a community-service project is a good idea, but helping others is as easy as saying hello, holding a door or volunteering to keep a neighbour's pet.

11. Learn ways to better deal with anger

It is totally normal to be angry sometimes – everyone gets mad at some point. The important thing is to deal with your anger in a healthy way. Cool down first and then focus on positive solutions to problems. This will help you to communicate better with the people in your life, and you can even earn more respect along the way. The next time something really has you stressed out, try these steps:

- Try to calm yourself down before doing or saying anything (counting to ten can help).
- Tell the other person what the problem is and how it makes you feel.
- Think of some solutions. What would the good and bad results of those solutions be?
- Explain your solution to the person you are upset with and try to put it into action together.

Hints to avoid harmful stress

We have discussed how stress can be harmful. So one activity worth spending time on is to consider how to reduce the impact of stressful situations

1. Work out priorities

Keep a list – make the tasks possible. Prioritise the tasks in order of importance and tick them off when done. Include the important people in your life as priorities and attend to these relationships first.

2. Identify your stress situations

Make a list of events that leave you emotionally drained, with one or two ways to reduce the stress for each. When they occur, use them as an opportunity to practise your stress-reduction techniques and keep notes on what works for next time.

3. Don't react to imagined insults

It is a waste of time and energy to be oversensitive to imagined insults, innuendo or sarcasm. Give people the benefit of the doubt; talk over the situation with someone you trust. They may have another spin on what was said.

4. Think before you commit

People can often perform tasks merely to feel accepted or liked by other people. Practice saying no to requests that are unreasonable or more than you can handle at the time, rather than suffer subsequent regrets and stress.

5. Move on: Don't dwell on past mistakes

Feelings of guilt, remorse and regret cannot change the past, and they make the present difficult by sapping your energy. Make a conscious effort to do something to change the mood (*eg* employ mindfulness techniques or do something active that you enjoy) when you feel yourself drifting into regrets about past actions. Learn from it and have strategies in place for next time. Learn to forgive yourself for past mistakes.

6. Don't bottle up anger & frustrations

Express and discuss your feelings to the person responsible for your agitation. If it is impossible to talk it out, plan for some physical activity at the end of the working day to relieve tensions. Let go of grudges – they affect you and your state of mind more than the other person.

7. Set aside time each day for recreation and exercise

Gentle repetitive exercise, such as walking, swimming or cycling, are good to relieve stress. Meditation, yoga, pilates and dance are also excellent. The trick is to find what suits you best. Hobbies that focus attention are also good stress relievers. Take up a new activity unrelated to teaching; one that gives you a sense of achievement and satisfaction. Establish new friends in your newly found interest.

8. Take your time

Frenzied activities lead to errors, regrets and stress. Request time to orient yourself to the situation. At work, if rushed, ask people to wait until you have finished working or thinking something out. Plan ahead to arrive at appointments early, composed and having made allowances for unexpected hold-ups. Practice approaching situations 'mindfully'.

9. Don't be aggressive on the road

Develop an 'I will not be ruffled' attitude. Drive defensively and give way to bullies. Near misses cause stress and strain, so does the fear of being caught for speeding. If possible, avoid peak hour traffic. If caught in it, relax by concentrating on deep (stomach) breathing or 'mindful driving'. Advanced driving lessons can also be useful.

10. Help children and young people to cope with stress

Children need the experience of being confronted with problems to try out, and to improve their ability to cope. By being overprotective or by intervening too soon, parents and teachers may prevent young people from developing valuable tolerance levels for problems, or from acquiring problem-solving skills.

11. Think positively

Smile whenever possible – it's an inexpensive and effective way of improving how you feel. Try and find something positive to say about a situation, particularly if you are going to find fault. You can visualise situations you have handled well, and hold those memories in your mind when going into stressful situations.

12. Cut down on drinking, smoking, sedatives & stimulants

These vices only offer temporary relief and don't solve the wider problem. Indeed, they can create more problems in terms of physical and mental health. Consider the effects you are looking for (sedation or stimulation) and how else you can achieve them.

Stress Management: challenges in the workplace for people leaders

Pressure is inevitable. In the workplace, it can be a source of positive motivation to succeed or it can be an overwhelming dark cloud that hinders morale, relationships and performance.

The rapid pace of changes in school structures, the need to adapt to changes to public policy, training provision, academisation, financial & budget constraints and the reduced role of local authorities have led to a range of stressors which we at the Education Support Partnership often hear of such as;

- Excessive workload/working hours
- Lack of control over workload

- Work schedule, inflexible work patterns, unreasonable expectations, allocation of directed time
- Inadequate employee participation in decision making
- Uncertainty about roles and responsibilities
- Inadequate consultation arrangements
- Inadequate training for teaching/non-teaching or management tasks
- Uncertain career development
- Organisational change and implementation of new policies and initiatives
- Inter-personal relationships at work such as poor or deteriorating relationship with immediate line manager
- Poor physical working conditions/environment
- Conflicting demands of work and home
- Lack of support at work and/or home
- Disruptive pupils
- Poor communication
- Aggressive pupils and parents
- Poorly handled monitoring and inspection

Levels of Stress

Stress

Stress is a normal, physiological adaptation to change. Healthy stress serves as a motivational drive to survive and succeed. When people are stressed, say by hunger, they act to relieve the stress by finding food and eating. When people are stressed by feelings of financial insecurity, they work hard to make sure they can provide for themselves and their families.

Distress

Distress is a destructive form of stress. Distress can manifest itself as high blood pressure, insomnia, irritability and poor job performance. During periods of distress, people often overreact and engage in self-defeating behaviours – like drinking too much, or driving too fast and having an accident.

Overload

Overload, often called burnout, results from long-term exposure to distress.

Overload causes exhaustion and fatigue, depression, accidents and poor job performance. Working long hours for an extended time or for many months without days off to recuperate are common causes.

Productivity versus Overload Stress brings both positive and negative aspects to the workplace. Providing for families, getting a promotion and making more money are all normal stresses that can motivate employees and increase productivity. Conversely, when stress becomes severe or overwhelming, worker morale and productivity declines. Through effective training and communication, good managers can learn to recognise the sources and signs of stress and can create a balance of healthy stress, opportunity and encouragement.

Sources of Stress in the workplace

Keep in mind that what motivates one worker may overwhelm another. Be aware of what happens outside the workplace. Stresses from home and other outside sources can dramatically affect productivity and morale. The causes of stress generally come from three sources:

1. An uncontrollable or unpredictable event. This might include a serious accident, the loss of a loved one or a sudden job change.

2. Being overwhelmed. Too many things can be on someone's plate at once, or things come at one too fast.

3. People working beyond their capabilities, skill level or coping resources. Common examples are taking on a new job without proper training, parenting stepchildren or caring for an elderly parent.

Signs and Symptoms of Workplace Stress

Signs an employee may be stressed include:

- withdrawal from others
- increased accidents, incidents and errors;
- increased absenteeism or lateness;
- more frequent illness and visits to the doctor;
- emotional outbursts;
- easily upset or angered;
- increased use of alcohol or other drugs.

Lighten the load

In today's fast-paced economy, the pressure to overwork and produce beyond prior limitations is constant, and in no sector more so than education. Understanding that humans need time to recuperate and recharge their batteries is central to reducing stress in the workplace. Organisations that fail to recognise the need for recuperation spend valuable time and capital addressing the symptoms of overload, which, in the long run, is counterproductive. (See Robin Bevan's chapter for some specific tools used in his school.)

Tips for managers to help reduce workplace stress

- Recognise the signs.
- Encourage employees to periodically 'unplug' from workplace stress by making the most of holiday time. Research by City University has recently proven that this down time is critical to building resilience and reductions in workplace strain. Try not to add more work during this time, and think carefully about when you send emails.
- Consider establishing the Education Support Partnership's employee assistance programme at school to support staff with stress-related or personal problems.
- Encourage continuing professional development – see Heath Monk's chapter for more suggestions
- Plan monthly 'stress busters', such as team members' birthday or length-of-service parties, stress-reduction workshops and motivational speakers
- Be quick to praise right thinking and initiative.
- When confrontation is necessary, do so in private, stick to performance issues and never admonish the person.

Time Management

Whether it is preparing students, organising logistics or tackling exam paperwork, managing your time as a teacher can be incredibly challenging. That's why we asked the Association of Professional Declutterers and Organisers (APDO) for their advice on how to stay organised.

Managing your Time

Successful teachers learn to say "no" in a positive way and limit their commitments, so that they can focus on their priorities. For many, balancing home and work will prove a problem from time to time. Discuss this with your line manager or another colleague. It is in your organisation's interest to help you find ways to manage your workload, rather than let it get out of control.

If you have a project to work on, start well in advance and plan your approach. Be realistic and spread the required work over some weeks. Plan your breaks and stick to the objective during work time. Do not drift into the depths of Google. If you are struggling to find a time and place where you won't be interrupted, put a 'Do not Disturb' sign on the door

Organising your paperwork

Owner of Organised Spaces, Samantha Bickerton, used to be a teacher in Further Education and Higher Education and still tutors today. She is naturally very organised but still found it challenging to keep on top of everything as a teacher. She found colour coding helpful: *"Colour code your storage to find things more quickly, eg by subject, theme, year group, or level, etc. Consider a range of colours when choosing storage or use large coloured stickers for existing storage."* Lever-arch and box files can also be helpful to separate different resource types.

It helps to use shelving with adjustable shelves to accommodate different storage solutions. The folders themselves should also be organised: *"It is quicker to find paperwork organised in smaller sections than to rummage through large boxes. Organise resources into lever-arch files labelled alphabetically. Inside the folders, use coloured dividers to divide alphabetically and use stamped poly pockets to hold resources with a sticker identifying the theme."*

Put time in your diary each day (or if this isn't feasible, each week) to move paperwork from your 'to file' folder into the relevant place in your filing system. On the computer, use folders to organise work in the same way – by year group, subject, theme, *etc*. Include the date in the file name so they're easier to find.

All of this can be terribly addictive, so it's important to focus on the end goal and prioritise function over aesthetics. *"Functional is a good starting point and can change your life, regardless of how it looks,"* says Bickerton.

Separating home and work

It's important to have time away from the stresses of work. The break will clear your head, give you perspective and make you more productive during the workday. Keep confidential papers and marking at work if at all possible – just don't take them home. If you must do so, define how long you will spend on it, where you will work and when you will stop – and stick to these limits. Make sure you give yourself time to wind down before bed.

Rachel Papworth, owner of decluttering company Green and Tidy says *"If you use a personal laptop for work, set up a separate user profile. This reduces the risk that you'll inadvertently show something personal to colleagues or students. Also, check your social media settings and make sure your pages are set to private. You can be sure that older students will check you out online."*

Getting enough rest

Everybody copes better with stress if they have had enough sleep. As well as winding down an hour or two before bed, make your bedroom a nice place to retreat to and ban any paperwork or digital devices. If you're struggling to clear your mind, try planning every day in advance with a list. You can tick things off the next day (increasing your own sense of achievement), and it will ease your worry that you will forget something.

During the day, plan and take regular breaks. Make a sandwich and cup of tea every day at lunchtime and tell students they can only speak to you after this time. Your holidays are not just a time to do everything that you haven't been able to fit in during term time. Papworth says: *"Plan your holidays in the same way you plan your work schedule: be realistic about how much you can fit in."* Rest and recuperation should also be included. You'll be back at work before you know it.

Time savers

Look out for little tricks during the day that will save you time, stress and energy. Invest in a cleaner, or ask members of the family to help out with household chores so you're not worrying about fitting them in. Filling a slow cooker in the morning will make evening meals much easier, and try not to put off tidying up jobs that will take a few minutes in the evening as you watch TV. Being organised will help enormously. Keep anything important on a USB drive that you can always have on you.

It's never been tougher to stay positive given the rapid pace of change and increasing number of responsibilities laid at the door of those in education but with the right help and support everyone can still aim to be at their best, to stay well and as a result to teach well.

Leading with workload in mind

An interview with Robin Bevan

Robin Bevan is an established school leader, with fifteen years secondary SLT experience in Essex schools. He has been Headteacher of a selective boys school in Southend for the last eight years. The 11-18 school has 1200 pupils on roll, making it 'slightly larger than the average secondary school' (according to his most recent Ofsted report).

Despite the selective intake, the school draws heavily from the local urban population. As a result the school community is culturally diverse, with significant variations in the home circumstances of those who attend. (The school is ranked just above the national median on socio-economic indicators.)

The school maintains a national profile, not least through its extensive and highly successful extra-curricular provision that includes an emphasis on sport, music, art, science/technology and languages.

As such, neither the school he leads nor the pressures he and the school faces are necessarily typical of all schools in the country. Robin is the first to point out that all schools are different, and that his could be viewed as in a more privileged position than some. However, he and his staff still face many workload pressures, not least as the institution is funded at a rate that places it in the lowest 10% of secondary schools in the country.

Robin has spoken at conferences, and recently at the Education Select Committee, about teacher workload, its impact on staff and pupils, and ways that he and his leadership team have developed over time to monitor and manage workload. In this interview, I have asked him to share some of those tools and practices. Some may be useful for other schools to use, some may be adaptable in other contexts and still others may prompt reflection on different ways to accomplish the same aims. I began by asking him about monitoring workload.

Nansi: How do you know what your staff workload is like, and how do you monitor that over time?

Robin: We use two different tools for that, aside from simply the obvious awareness of the workload that's associated with significant change and clearly that varies year-on year. One of the most useful tools that we've developed was a tool that we first used simply as a means of discriminating between those colleagues who were genuinely hard pressed and those who just made a lot of noise about it! What we did was we plotted onto a graph the total number of different individual pupils a particular teacher would see across a fortnight (our timetable is organised in fortnightly blocks), so if they saw a lot of classes, a lot of large classes, at Key Stage 3 for one or two periods across a fortnight that means a lot of report writing, different names to learn, it does generate a particular kind of workload. And on the other axis we plotted their total throughput so if you had ten lessons each with 30 pupils in that period that would give you a score of 300 and that allowed us to take account of those members of staff who had large A level classes for example, or large classes in option subjects in contrast to those who have smaller classes where their option is perhaps less popular. We plotted those against each other and drew a boundary curve which represented our sense of what the upper limit of a reasonable workload was at that time.

In 2011/12 when we did it (see figure 1), we just had a few colleagues above that boundary line and we were able then to make some adjustments to the way we worked with those colleagues. These weren't huge structural adjustments, more recognising that we had colleagues who would need a little more tolerance when it came to some of the workload expectations.

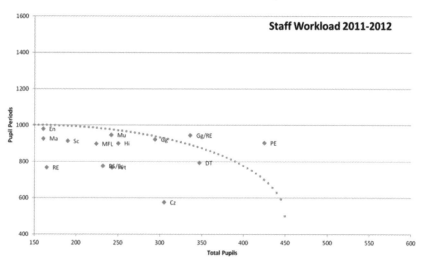

Figure 1

We found that this was so helpful that we repeated the exercise each year for several years, and the striking feature in terms of the 2015/16 situation is that across a period in which funding has forced us to increase class sizes and reduce sixth form contact time, and therefore increase the number of different classes that colleagues are seeing, we've seen a very significant shift in the number of colleagues who are beyond that prior boundary line (see figure 2). It's a kind of way of measuring workload that's often hidden in secondary schools, it highlights the comparative workload of PE teachers who tend to have a large throughput of different students and perhaps your maths department where teachers see a narrower range of individual students but, because they see them more often, tend to have a larger workload associated with the pupil period count. We have used that to make decisions about form-tutoring for example, so some of these teachers with very significantly heavy workload are relieved of their form tutor duties a couple of days a week. We've not been able to do much more than that, but we do recognise that this is an insight into the authentic experience of those colleagues in raw pupil-teaching terms.

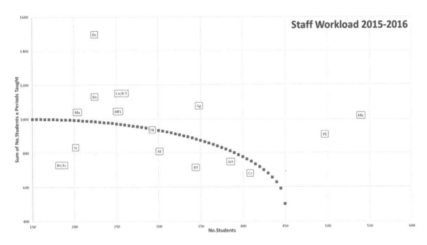

Figure 2

There's a second tool that we use (figure 3) which is about the distribution of the expectations that are placed on our colleagues. We've done this using an annual bar chart. Against each week of the school year we give a block of time assigned to the various tasks that a teacher might reasonably be expected to do on top of their routine teaching, marking and preparation so the items that we log are parents evenings, report writing, interim grades – like most schools we have a broadly termly monitoring programme of pupil progress – and we've recently added into it the production of UCAS submissions where we have a large number of staff who do sixth form reports at that time as well. For each of those if, for example, the deadline for reports was in week 18 we would allocate a couple of hours in week 16 and 17 for the purpose of writing those reports. So this is, if you like, 'out of hours' work for colleagues.

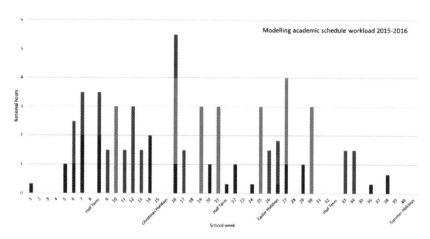

Figure 3

When we first did it, we became acutely aware that the schedule that we'd created was very uneven. There were things we could do about it so our first response was to relocate some of those items, although our feeling is that in the beginning of the spring term there will be a number of coinciding deadlines that will be difficult to move. The second thing that we did was we realised that there tends to be a peak in the second or third week after the half term holidays. This might be associated in the summer with exam classes, or in the spring term with report writing for exam classes. We made a decision based on that to modify our expectation for teachers in terms of setting homework for that time. We actually declared a Key Stage 3 'no-homework-zone' for the week immediately after half term which then of course means no marking of that homework for those teachers in the second and third week after half term.

Every year, because the school year changes, we have to redesign that schedule and teachers have become quite used to the model that we use. The expectation that they will plan their workload across the week or fortnight before deadlines helps them not to leave everything to the last minute.

Nansi: What problems do you encounter that you would say are down to heavy workload?

Robin: There are several dimensions here. First there are those that arise that are just to do with working with human beings. Colleagues can respond in very different ways when their workload is close to being unsustainable and indeed when it crosses that threshold. There's no doubt that there are a lot of teachers in schools, partly because they are self-driven and partly because of the system, who find themselves around that boundary line. (Julian Stanley's chapter gives pointers to identify colleagues experiencing pressure and stress.) I guess the first response is to recognise that as teachers' workload increases, those elements that are associated with human welfare increase. There are colleagues who hide their difficulties, there are colleagues who will just stop as a result of the challenges they're facing and effectively manage it themselves, there are other colleagues who if you're not careful will give you an absence problem not far down the line if you're not aware of what they're doing. So in response to the human issues the very first and most important response is to make sure they're in a working environment where people can talk openly and honestly about their workload and about how they're feeling about their workload. Sometimes the perception and the reality are very different, and how they feel about it is really important to understand.

The second, and this has become a bigger issue for us over the past two or three years, is that as workload increases the capacity for new developments declines. And yet it is working on new, sometimes creative, sometimes technological or pedagogical, initiatives that often gives teachers their enthusiasm. That question 'What are you working on this year?' historically has been greeted with energy and passion, but as workload increases that tends to be dominated by items that are a measure of compulsion or requirement. (See Heath Monk's chapter on CPD.) So you then get those very difficult decisions about which initiatives to support, what can be ignored, what can be delayed, and certainly within my own school we are having to park a number of quite exciting developments that we want to do as we don't know when we'll have a receptive audience.

I think the third element is associated with the quality of delivery. As workload increases, the capacity to respond creatively to lesson planning declines. There is no doubt as well that the capacity to differentiate effectively creates further workload; and with a large class that is an obvious impact on individual students' needs. There's also an overlap with the human dimension: as workload increases and colleagues sense the pressure of that workload, we have to work very hard to ensure that pressure is not transmitted to the students. And indeed we, once again, have had open conversations with the staff about ensuring that any pressure that they are experiencing is not transmitted to the students in their care. That's difficult but it's a very key issue associated with workload.

Nansi: So what do you do to support your staff?

Robin: In terms of supporting staff there are three different strategies that we have used. There are two that are associated with the culture of a school, the climate of a school: when we see the difficulties that arise because of workload, if the solutions are only practical then they tend not to address the human and interpersonal issues. So the first strategy that we've used widely now is based on Professor Viviane Robinson's work 'Open to learning conversations'[52]. The key part of her work is that if you are facing a difficulty or if there's an issue in your workplace (just a day-to-day issue) that you address the problem directly with the person who is responsible for that area rather than moaning with twenty other colleagues first. Then, when you present it, you expect to have in response a colleague who will listen without judgment, then present their view of the situation, and that you will then work together on a solution. Our work in this area we feel has not only helped colleagues with their workload but has also increased the speed with which decisions can be made in the organisation in general.

We've also, as a second tool, introduced an element associated with wellbeing to the performance management process. Performance management can be challenging for some colleagues: by its very nature we can be involved in conversations where we're telling colleagues that they've not performed in some areas as well as they might do, but we're also giving them very encouraging messages. Within that process we identified ten factors which have been adapted from the work of writers such as Stephen Covey, ten factors that contribute to an open, healthy, constructive, happy workplace (see figure 4). There's no doubt that when colleagues are feeling comfortable in a workplace they will sustain a higher level of workload at least for a period. For each of those ten dimensions we've highlighted what they look like when they are effectively deployed.

For example, when you're given a high level of permission in a workplace to get on with your own work it can lead to intelligent, responsible decision making. On the other hand it is possible, with insufficient permission, to leave colleagues unable to use their own professional judgement or, at the other end of the scale with too much permission, they can feel that they are lacking guidance, and in particular they may feel that they have to do everything and they're unable to limit the pressure on themselves to just a few priorities. So we take each of those ten dimensions and in every performance management conversation with teachers and support staff a conversation takes place in which the colleague is asked to identify any area in which they feel the team is working particularly well and any where they would welcome a little more clarity, freedom, appreciation or whatever it may be.

---

52 See for example www.youtube.com/watch?v=o_l5-HKIR1s and www.bastow.vic.edu.au/ courses/open-to-learning-leadership

effectively deployed if	dimension	unproductive when
colleagues are able to fulfil their roles knowing exactly what is needed and when, with the 'tools' and resources readily available	clarity	the level and detail of instruction is out of proportion to the task or becomes micro-management; or when explanations don't need to be part of the message
colleagues are confident about communicating clearly to the relevant person about issues within their working lives or environment	assertion	statements are made without the possibility of there being an alternative view; or no time is afforded for a reasonable response; or commentary is offered on another colleague's competence
colleagues are ready to listen and consider alternatives (from any source) and willing to contribute freely to improvements (in any area)	openness	positive suggestions are presented as critical evaluation; or the rejection of an idea is taken as a personal slight or closure to further suggestions
colleagues are assumed to understand, know and be able to fulfil their responsibilities; colleagues recognise the constructive place for monitoring and evaluating approaches and outcomes	trust	trust is confused with a lack of support, trust is used to justify a lack of clarity or resources; or monitoring becomes viewed as interference and evaluation as 'assumed criticism'
colleagues know the extent to which they have flexibility to make decisions about their working practices and are free to make responsible choices	permission	the freedom to adapt individual working patterns becomes an opportunity to 'do less'; or judgements are made about other colleague's dedication or diligence on the basis of their choices
colleagues apply the highest standards of integrity and judgement within the freedom of their role	professionalism	professional status or position is confused with superiority; or standards are applied to others that are not reflected in our own conduct
colleagues are able to regulate their own workload, manage their own pressures, plan for the known demands and accommodate the unexpected demands of their role	self-responsibility	the opportunity to be 'in control' and the benefits of 'self-regulation' become an excuse to allow others to 'flounder'
colleagues are mindful of the well-being of all those around them: not escalating 'pressure' or conflict, easing the way to be managed by others, helping others to follow when being led	regard for others	concern for others extends to intrusion; welfare becomes a source of gossip; passivity prevents progress; kindness inhibits challenge; empathy tolerates under-performance

effectively deployed if	dimension	unproductive when
colleagues recognise the efforts and contributions of those around them, even when the task or role is routine; saying 'thank you'	appreciation	thanks are expressed only in recognition of public or special efforts, or used to flatter the recipient into accepting further demands
colleagues respond to challenges with a 'can-do' ethos, differentiating successfully between what can be changed and what is inevitable, and helping others to do the same	positivity	abnormal pressures go unnoticed or unsupported; insensitivity fails to identify and take action on key issues of difficulty

Figure 4

On a more practical note we have also encouraged those colleagues who feel close to their limit to actually stop some of the tasks that they are doing for a limited period. When you encounter a teacher who tells you that their current workload is unsustainable and you know that they are a hard worker who is not making this comment lightly, then as a leader you cannot hear that comment and let them carry on. You have to provide them with some alleviation. So for example, we have said to colleagues on occasion that they should simply stop marking, have a week off marking, and then not try and catch up subsequently. Simply to take one week when they go home early and recharge their batteries. Within the school as a whole we've seen very significant benefits from this, not only in welfare and capacity to handle work, but also very significant reductions in staff sickness absence with on average, last year, teaching colleagues taking one day off in the whole year.

Nansi: What do you see as the drivers of this workload?

Robin: There's no doubt that the most significant drivers for us in the last couple of years have been curriculum reform and financial constraints. I'm well aware that there are other drivers that will affect other schools in other contexts and perhaps in different ways. For example, reductions in income and our desire to remain financially viable have forced us to increase class sizes in sixth form by 50% and lower down the school by 15% or thereabouts. Cumulatively that has a very significant effect. We've also increased the size of our year groups, so pastoral leaders have more responsibility that they had before, without any significant increase in resources to support them.

Second to that is curriculum reform: curriculum reform that has not been resourced, not been sufficiently notified, and even though we knew it was coming we didn't have the final details. This curriculum reform is wholesale even though in some instances it only gives rise to marginal differences. So in some subjects, in A level history for example, we have some teachers who are having to learn a whole new period of history which they have never studied previously though they have for many years been expert A level teachers. They are teaching these subjects without having access to published text books, or at least course specific textbooks, and are having to do this for A level while simultaneously having to teach a brand new GCSE course which we have had to guess the content of because of the pathway our year 9 and indeed year 10 students follow. In contrast, the maths department is not anticipating significant changes in content of the A level course, and the GCSE course is already up and running with some changes. But the very fact that module boundaries are changing yet again, and the composition of papers is changing yet again, has a significant bearing on where time is being spent.

It's worth bearing in mind that the most productive I've ever seen the teaching staff working is with a period of curriculum stability. Typically, it's in the third year of a new course that teachers move from first delivery and structural refinement to genuine pedagogical refinement – 'This didn't work terribly well, how can we do it better next time?' or 'Our students never seem to understand this, what alternatives can we apply?' That can only happen in those periods of stability.

There have been other sources of increased workload. We're not the only school to struggle to recruit teachers into certain areas, and personally I have had to teach subjects that are not my specialist subject. I know that I can prepare a high quality maths lesson with about 15 minutes preparation for an hour's lesson: I've taken over an hour to prepare a business studies lesson of an hour's duration. I'm perfectly capable and competent but simply unfamiliar with the content, having to find for the first time new examples of relevant material. This is happening increasingly as teachers are having to teach outside their specialism, and it has a major impact on workload.

Nansi: Finally, Robin, how do you manage your own workload, and how does your governing board help you with managing both your own and your colleagues' workload?

Robin: For my own workload, I was challenged recently at a conference I attended by a lecturer, Dr Karen Edge, who asked us as senior managers whether we conduct our work in ways that make the job look attractive. Leaders must make it look attractive if we want teachers to follow us into leadership roles, just as teachers must make it look attractive to students – or we won't sustain the high levels of teacher recruitment that we need. In a personal capacity, I make good use of support staff, and I use effective time management techniques. Being responsible for colleagues, as far as possible I give them freedom to do their jobs, and ask them to let me know if there are problems.

Not only do I believe it's important to demonstrate that the job is sustainable and enjoyable, but I also try to be visible in participating with students and colleagues in appropriate contexts – so we're working hard, but we're enjoying social and relaxation activities too.

As a result of our planning and mapping exercises, I've been looking at workload with the senior leadership team. I've told people that there is no need for them to attend meetings if there's no relationship with the job that they're doing, for example.

As for the governing board, we try to make sure that the meetings happen at critical points for decision-making. I am very clear that we don't generate paperwork for the governing board that doesn't already exist. Two of our subcommittees regularly ask questions about staff workload: when we discuss curriculum and pupil matters they routinely ask about the impact of staff workload on pupils, and for example the impact of curriculum changes on staff capacity. The human resources committee uses the monitoring tools, monitors staff absence and indicators of well-being in the workplace. It keeps a focus on issues of well-being and mental health in the workplace – and we have a separate policy for mental health, as well as providing access to occupational health advice where it's needed. (And see Emma Knights' chapter for more information on governing boards.)

As a school, we have a well-being programme for all colleagues. There are opportunities available, once every three weeks, which have included yoga, a curry night and a bike ride.

The chair of the governing board asks me routinely, as headteacher, about my personal circumstances, how I'm managing demands on my own time, and about life outside school. The chair also recognises the limits on my capacity to do or respond to everything. A good chair will give permission to the headteacher not to do everything.

Nansi: Thank you Robin, for a very useful insight into the ways in which your school is working to help staff to reduce the pressures of workload.

Takeaway

Although many pressures on your time come from national changes there are things that can be done at school level to manage that.

Open and trusting workplaces are better able to come up with solutions and while this is often driven by the leadership, everyone has some responsibility.

Questions:

What tools does your school use for monitoring workload – both 'in-class' and 'out-of-hours'? Can you work together to develop some if you don't have any?

How far is your school climate one of trust and openness? How far do you feel able to raise concerns about workload with your line manager? With colleagues? What steps could you take to improve this?

Are there tasks that you could just stop, for a period or for longer, so that you can lower your stress levels?

Does your school have a well-being programme? Could you work with colleagues (and your unions) to develop one?

Tackling workload together – creating a healthy workplace

Collette Bradford

"It's not enough to be busy, so are the ants.
The question is what are we busy about?"

Henry David Thoreau

The key drivers of excessive workload and working hours are school and college wide.

An ATL workload survey (2015) found that eight out of ten drivers of workload originate at workplace level. The survey also found that the top five tasks that members felt they should be doing less of were also managed at workplace level: fewer meetings, less administration, being able to choose how and when to mark, fewer cover duties including lunchtime supervision along with a more measured approach in the workplace to inspection, observation and the appraisal process.

The same survey of teachers, leaders and support staff found that over 70% thought that improved consultation and dialogue between staff and leaders on how to reduce workload in their workplace would be helpful; and over 80% said that having an appraisal target to reduce workload would help them to focus on improving their work-life balance.

For many education professionals, the reality is work spills over into their weekend, causing conflicts with other life responsibilities, with their health and with their family.

Tackling workload at workplace level collaboratively can make a real difference to how people feel about their workplace and improve well-being. Many ATL/ AMiE reps and members have taken the lead in tackling work-life balance in their schools and colleges with great success. You and your colleagues will know what works best in your school or college, and what is practically possible.

Some changes can be fairly simple, such as agreeing to reduce the length of time of a meeting so everyone can go home 20 minutes early; others, such as developing a new marking policy, are going to be more complex.

Any actions taken to tackle workload, reduce working hours and improve work-life balance will be more effective if taken collectively, across the whole workplace, with staff and leaders working collaboratively to make positive changes. The changes aim to free up more time for what is important – teaching and learning – and to improve the well-being of staff and the learning experience of students.

Building a case for change

Leaders, teachers, lecturers and support staff working collaboratively to make real changes in their workplace to reduce their workload and improve their work-life balance has a positive impact on the culture of their school/college, the quality of the teaching and the overall learning experience of the children and young people they teach and support. Each time a workplace problem is explored, resolved together or an agreed change implemented, the experience strengthens the workplace team, empowers staff and develops organisational capacity to deal with other workload and well-being challenges.

Benefits for education employers and leaders

- Reduces work-place and sector stress
- Raises morale
- Makes for healthy workforce and happy classrooms
- Improves relationships and supports staff development
- Focuses on what's important in teaching & learning
- Improves retention and impacts positively on recruitment of new staff
- Impacts on budgets – is cost effective in the longer term

Benefits for education employees

- Reduces stress
- Raises morale
- Results in employees feeling valued and having a better life balance
- Improves health, wellbeing and happiness
- Realigns the focus on teaching & learning
- Allows time for employees to develop – relationships, knowledge & practice
- Increases career opportunities, and helps employees stay in education longer

What the law says

Employers have a legal and moral duty to protect the health, safety and welfare of its staff. There is a wealth of legislation imposing certain requirements and responsibilities on employers including the Health and Safety at Work Act 1974, the Management of Health and Safety Regulations 1999, the Working Time Regulations 1998, the Disability Discrimination Act 1995. In addition, there is the employer's duty of care established by common law to ensure employees are not exposed to unnecessary risks to their health along with codes of practice to give employers practical ways of reducing the risks.

What makes a healthy workplace?

Leaders and managers have a responsibility to support healthy workplaces to monitor workloads, working time and working practices and ensure good communications with staff.

All staff members have the responsibility to report any issues in relation to workload, wellbeing and stress and to work together with leaders to develop a healthy workplace though good communication and by finding solutions to issues together. Good relationships have the potential to make workplaces healthy and productive.

ACAS, the Advisory, Conciliation and Arbitration Service, produces useful guidance on healthy workplaces. While this was traditionally focussed on 'health and safety', they now consider the relationship between jobs and mental and physical wellbeing[53].

Good employment relations are built on effective policies for managing people issues (such as communication, absence, grievance and occupational health) and high levels of trust between employees and managers, for instance where workers are involved in decision-making and finding solutions to workplace problems.

Other features that you may find in a healthy workplace include:

- line managers who are confident and trained in people skills
- an organisation where you feel valued and involved in decisions
- the use of appropriate health services (*eg* occupational health where practicable) to tackle absence and help you get back to work
- managers who promote an attendance culture
- flexible and well-designed jobs

---

53 www.acas.org.uk/index.aspx?articleid=1972

- managers who identify problems at an early stage and seek to resolve them using informal methods
- managers who know how to manage common health problems such as mental health and musculoskeletal disorders (MSDs).

Where to begin?

You don't need to know all the answers to begin asking the right questions in order to initiate conversations with colleagues about workload and its impact on them and their students or to begin to explore potential solutions.

You could make notes from the conversations you have together or you could use a tool such as the ATL workload tracker[54] or a workplace questionnaire designed with others to collate the evidence you will need.

In addition to collating the evidence about the issues you should also collate evidence about the impact it has on staff and on pupils.

It is also worth spending some time reflecting on the weight of that evidence, the strength of staff feeling and the likelihood of success in achieving change together.

If you have a structure for staff consultation in your workplace, prepare to raise the issues at your joint negotiating committee or joint consultative committee, or other relevant staff committees (*eg* health and safety or monthly staff meeting).

If there is no consultation forum for staff reps and leaders in your school/ college, consider asking for one and establishing a regular consultation meeting to open the lines of communication about the issues you face in your workplace and to explore positive solutions together.

A framework to help get you started

This framework takes you through a number of ways in which you can identify the problems you face and the likelihood of success of any campaign to resolve them. While it focuses on workload, these methods can be used to tackle a variety of issues in your workplace.

The first step is to discuss the issue with your union reps. If there is no rep or contact in your workplace, decide who will take on this role (this can be more than one person).

---

54 www.atl.org.uk/abouttime

Assessing the viability of a workload campaign in your workplace

You and your colleagues could use the following checklist.

Will the issue of workload:

- be widely felt by colleagues?
- be deeply felt by colleagues?
- be winnable or partly winnable? Explore solutions.
- result in a real improvement on the lives of colleagues if change is achieved?
- be easy to understand by all involved?
- bring staff together?
- increase the visibility of your union/ your campaign?

You should also consider if there are there other reasons why it would be good to organise around this issue.

Putting the plan together

Once you've assessed the strength of the workload issue in your workplace, the following general *'problem, information, plan'* approach is a useful way to help develop a plan to tackle this issue.

Problem, information, plan (PIP) checklist

Problem

- ☐ Identify the problem – what is it?
- ☐ What are the causes?
- ☐ Why is it a problem?
- ☐ What is the impact?
- ☐ Have you spoken to colleagues who are concerned?
- ☐ Is it an individual problem, collective problem or both?
- ☐ Is it partly or wholly an issue which can be dealt with at workplace level?

Information

- ☐ What information do you need?
- ☐ How can you get information from the employer and other organisations?
- ☐ How can the government's workload working group reports help? See the chapters from Nansi Ellis and Mary Myatt

- ☐ Does your union have work-life resources?
- ☐ What do your workplace / local / national agreements say?
- ☐ What do your terms and conditions of employment say?
- ☐ Is there any relevant procedure or employer policy?
- ☐ Is the problem covered by law?
  - · Health & safety
  - · Employment
  - · Equality
- ☐ What is the advice from the unions?
- ☐ Has it happened before and what was the outcome?
- ☐ Have other people tried to deal with this issue and how will you find out?
- ☐ What do other colleagues/members feel about the issue and would they support or get involved or help?
- ☐ Is there any other information you need?

Plan

- ☐ How will you tackle this issue together?
- ☐ What is/are the specific thing(s) you want to change?
- ☐ Who will you need to work with to resolve this issue?
- ☐ What avenues are there available to raise this issue in the workplace?
- ☐ What would be a realistic aim or approach?
- ☐ What advice, support, and assistance do you need from other reps, members, union district / branch?
- ☐ As you try to resolve the problem, what could you ask others to do to get them more involved?

Identifying the problem

The first thing to consider in your plan is how you can gather evidence about the scale of the workload issue and its impact.

The workload tracker on ATL's website (www.atl.org.uk/abouttime) is a useful resource to find out where colleagues are spending their time and on what.

Surveys and questionnaires which you can devise can help you identify and quantify the:

- work-life balance issues in your school/college
- key drivers of excessive workload in your workplace
- impact they have on staff
- impact they have on your students
- impact they have on the school/college

Identifying these drivers is an important step towards being able to develop practical solutions that when implemented reduce workload and create a healthier workplace to the benefit of staff and pupils.

Next steps

Thinking about the information and resources you have available to help you to solve the problem, you now have to decide where to focus.

What goal can you work on together? The first goal you choose may not help you solve everything, but will help you on your way to solving the problem, for example achieving a goal of securing regular consultation meetings with the senior leadership team on workload and well-being.

Once you have been successful in achieving your first goal, setting and achieving further goals will become easier. You will develop confidence through the process.

Things to consider

- Share the results of your surveys or the ATL workload tracker and/or any information with colleagues to demonstrate the drivers of excessive workload and its impact in your workplace and the students you teach.
- Involve your workplace union reps or if you are the school/college rep or contact, consider calling a members meeting to discuss the issue and gauge the strength of feeling.
- Identify volunteers to help collect and collate any further evidence and information from colleagues.
- Use the evidence you have collated to initiate a discussion with colleagues to explore solutions and concrete suggestions for changes in practice that will reduce workload.
- Have informal and creative discussions in the workplace, maybe during breaktimes or lunch periods, which are solution focused.
- Perhaps raise the issue at a suitable staff meeting or through other communication systems.
- Take a collaborative approach, using negotiation and consultation forums

to discuss the evidence and solutions with leaders.

· Invite leaders to contribute concerns about workload and reflect on reasons why certain practices take place.

· Prioritise the most important aspects, and work together to reach an agreement on practical steps which can be taken to reduce excessive workload and create a healthier, well workplace.

Consultation and collaboration is the key to success in tackling workload. Where possible, find case studies of successful work-life balance in other workplaces or examples of strategies implemented to reduce workload. These may carry weight with your leadership team and can be helpful in identifying examples of good practice and potential solutions.

This flowchart gives a different way of looking at possible activity towards reducing workload.

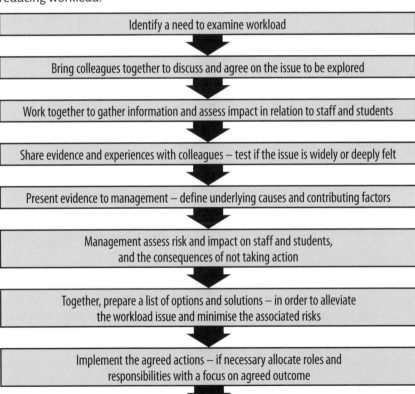

Identify a need to examine workload

Bring colleagues together to discuss and agree on the issue to be explored

Work together to gather information and assess impact in relation to staff and students

Share evidence and experiences with colleagues – test if the issue is widely or deeply felt

Present evidence to management – define underlying causes and contributing factors

Management assess risk and impact on staff and students, and the consequences of not taking action

Together, prepare a list of options and solutions – in order to alleviate the workload issue and minimise the associated risks

Implement the agreed actions – if necessary allocate roles and responsibilities with a focus on agreed outcome

Review together, report on success and learning – tweak as necessary and share with others

Taking action together for better work-life balance

Here are some general actions[55] you can take forward to discuss with leaders and managers in your school or college to begin to develop a focus for a better work-life balance and to open up dialogue on workload and well-being issues:

- find ways to promote the positive messages about supporting work-life balance to colleagues, staff and unions in the workplace *eg* #teachers5aday campaign
- develop or ask to review policies that acknowledge the association between work-related stress and mental health
- encourage and support a culture of openness about time constraints and workload and talk openly to colleagues. Staff must feel able to speak up (and know who to speak to) if the demands placed on them are too great
- support and encourage training for staff and managers (and H&S reps) on stress management so that they can spot stress, poor work-life balance and its effects on the individual and workplace
- promote a culture of 'working smart, not long' and be open and share when you do things differently
- leaders can ensure that employees' jobs are manageable within the time for which they are contracted *eg* part time colleagues and support staff
- encourage audits and staff surveys about work environments to identify elements of practice, policy or culture that may be detrimental to a healthy work-life balance and positive mental health management (and see Emma Knights' chapter about the duties of governing boards in supporting health and well-being)
- leaders can monitor and evaluate policies against performance indicators such as sickness, absence, staff retention and improvements in staff satisfaction and develop impact assessments for new policies that are introduced
- staff can be encouraged to make use of Employee Assistance Programmes (EAPs), occupational health and other support services during working hours
- encourage activities that promote good mental health such as regular breaks, making the most of non-contact time, opportunities to collaborate with colleagues, lunch time (reserved for eating lunch), the benefits of exercise and/or relaxation classes

---

55 Adapted from the AMiE publication Well-being: leading and managing a well workplace p.22 amie.atl.org.uk/wellworkplace

- organise a staff and student wellbeing day – to talk about issues of well-being and positive mental health; consider inviting other organisations into school/college to participate and to provide information and services to staff and students – be creative and get others involved

- use your union's resources to make contact with others in your area to share ideas and create a well-being network

- Take a look at the ATL campaign www.atl.org.uk/abouttime for more resources, information and case studies

- Use the workload working group reports to identify possible areas of focus.[56]

Takeaway

There are many workplace solutions to alleviate workload, reduce working hours and to improve work-life balance. Putting just a little time into finding out your workplace issues and deciding what solutions would benefit you is worth the effort in the longer term. Even small changes make a difference – try it and see!

---

56 www.gov.uk/government/publications/reducing-teachers-workload/reducing-teachers-workload

How can your governing board help reduce your workload?

Emma Knights

A duty of care

It may never have occurred to you that your governing board has a role to play in helping to reduce your workload. In fact, the governing board is either your employer or, in the case of community schools and voluntary controlled schools, acts as the employer on behalf of the local authority. Employers have a duty of care to their employees, which means that they should take all steps which are reasonably possible to ensure their health, safety and wellbeing.

Legally, employers must abide by relevant health & safety and employment law, as well as the common law duty of care. They also have a moral and ethical duty not to cause, or fail to prevent, physical or psychological injury, and must fulfil their responsibilities with regard to personal injury and negligence claims. Requirements under an employer's duty of care are wide-ranging but they are likely to include ensuring that staff do not work excessive hours and providing areas for rest and relaxation as well as providing communication channels for employees to raise concerns and consulting employees on issues of concern.

An employer can be deemed to have breached their duty of care by failing to do everything that was reasonable in the circumstances to keep the employee safe from harm. Employees also have responsibilities for their health and wellbeing at work – for example, they are entitled by law to refuse to undertake work that isn't safe without fear of disciplinary action.

Good places to work

Demonstrating concern for the physical and mental health of your workers shouldn't just be seen as a legal duty, it's also the right thing to do, the moral thing to do. Of course, those governing should never forget they act first and foremost in the interests of children, but there's a clear business reason to ensure the welfare of staff too. In these times of recruitment difficulties, the school's leadership needs to show it values staff in order to improve retention. Prioritising staff welfare is a key factor in building trust as well as reinforcing an employer's commitment to their employees. Research has demonstrated links between being happier in a job and being better at a job, and happy school staff are likely to make for happy pupils. Schools need to be good, vibrant places to work as well as to learn.

Governing boards across the country no doubt aspire to this, but I am not convinced that it has perhaps been systematically considered at school level. Most governors will be aware of the issue of increasing workload for teachers, particularly as a result of changes in the curriculum, qualifications and assessment. At the National Governors' Association (NGA) we aim to keep our members up to date, with not only those changes, but also relevant national developments, such as the DfE's workload survey and the subsequent working groups on marking, planning and data management. But significant numbers of governing boards have not signed up as members of NGA, and very few will read the education media, so some may well not be fully aware of increases in the workload and the stress brought about, in part because of the accountability system and changing curriculum and assessment.

Values & ethos

Of course the culture in schools is going to be affected by the national context, but we have perhaps been too quick to label the system as 'high stakes' and not to take responsibility as individual organisations for ensuring a healthy culture. Taking responsibility at all levels from the individual to leadership level is an essential pre-requisite to a healthy organisation. Being trapped in victim status is extremely disabling.

It is the governing board's responsibility to set those values and ethos, but they need to be owned and lived by all in the school, including the pupils. When were those values last considered, communicated and do they resonate with staff? Do they have any bearing on the issue of staff wellbeing? Are they visible in the conduct and decisions of governors and leaders? (See Lee Card's chapter for an example of this in practice.)

Culture and climate

The culture of an organisation should flow from its values and ethos, but only if they are meaningful and known by all in the school. Governing boards need to set those conditions which allow for a healthy culture, model the behaviours which will ensure that culture, hold leaders to account for inculcating the culture and understand the climate of their school.

The climate of any organisation will be affected by the extent to which it focuses on and emphasises appreciation and recognition, concern for employee well-being, learning and development, teamwork, leadership, involvement, empowerment, citizenship, ethics, quality performance, innovation and flexibility. Experience from all types of sectors seems to show that organisations with more progressive practices tend to outperform those with fewer.

Not all of this is written down in a school, and a culture, possibly developed over many years, might not always be perceived in the same way by everyone. It will usually be affected by a change of school leadership, but not to the same extent if the culture truly comes from the school's values and ethos which you would expect to stand the test of time. It certainly is affected by the mind-sets and behaviours of staff; there may be different perceptions about 'the way things get done around here'.

It is important to set aspirations that emphasise health as well as performance, but that does not mean change can be avoided. Staying healthy as an organisation does require constantly reviewing, adjusting and adapting to the changing times and challenges. Healthy organisations identify risks and recognise and seize opportunities. They never stop learning, and they support continuous improvement, not simply demand it. This requires investment in staff training and development, but also being responsive to the needs of your employees.

Healthy work environments motivate staff and continually prompt and emphasise constructive behaviours in the school: cheerfulness, kindness, respect, collaboration, appreciation, personal growth and working together to meet the objectives. Employees at healthy organisations learn from one another and help each other, and quickly recover when difficult situations or mistakes happen. They don't allow organisational 'wounds' such as poor performance to fester, but deal with them constructively.

Taking the temperature

The governing board therefore needs to be fully aware of the culture and climate at the school and must make sure they have ways of hearing from the school's staff. There are various ways this can be done. Informal discussions with staff, whether at events or alongside formal monitoring visits, can be useful indicators. Visiting the school is an important source of information for those governing, and can of course provide an inkling of the morale and culture.

However governors should not drift in and out of school, or become a frequent presence. Given that most governors are employed, visiting during school hours has to be done sparingly with real purpose. It may be to learn about the school, to discuss progress on priorities with staff, or to represent the governing board at school events. Often school staff would like governors to be more visible, but it is important that staff do understand the time constraints of those volunteering and the strategic nature of the role.

The chair and vice chairs will gain an impression from the headteacher which can be important, but will be less useful where the culture is not a healthy one which encourages honesty or the climate is deteriorating. Similarly the extent to which staff are able to be honest with governors and trustees is difficult; conversations which are trying to subvert usual management routes are not appropriate, and yet at the same time those governing need to understand if there are problems of culture and climate.

Off-the-record conversations are usually to be avoided; a culture of gossip, rumour and moaning is a clear sign of dysfunction, and governors must not encourage this behaviour. However all schools must have a whistle-blowing policy as well as a staff grievance process, and these must be known about by staff and issues dealt with fairly and professionally.

Perceptions of all staff should be formally gathered anonymously and considered regularly. Staff surveys are a standard tool which should be used in any organisation. A range of companies sell and administer staff surveys for schools and these have the benefit of benchmarking data, but experience tells us that the number of schools that undertake pupil and parent surveys substantially outweighs those that conduct teacher surveys.

Anecdotally, the reasons for this appear to be that school leaders are wary about what responses might be, given the large number of national changes that they have little control over. But without getting feedback from staff, it is almost impossible to fully understand what is happening in your school. So for those schools that cannot afford to buy a staff survey, one should be constructed and carried out in-house, with the results reported to the governing board, as well as of course the staff. Questions needs to be carefully constructed to obtain meaningful responses, and questions about workload must be included.

A survey which uncovers issues, which almost all do, will certainly require action by senior leaders, or may just require further monitoring by governors; however sometimes there may be significant issues which governors need to understand more fully and consider solutions.

One way is to hold a focus group of staff, the issue being discussed is likely to determine who is invited or it might be a random sample. Conducting such a focus group is a very skilled task, one which should be undertaken by a governor with relevant experience or after specific training. It can feel threatening to senior leaders who are likely to be concerned that their authority will be undermined. Such an exercise is very likely to uncover a range of perceptions, and people can experience the same situation, disagree at to what is going on and yet both be right. In order to get a balanced and objective view, governors need to listen to a range of other voices, not just the loudest ones, and be open to all. The views and needs of staff need to be set alongside the views and needs of parents and pupils.

Developing the school's strategic priorities

Every year the governing board should carry out an exercise to review the school's vision – where do we want to be in three or five years' time – and its strategic priorities – how are we going to get there and realise that vision. NGA has published with the Wellcome Trust the Framework for Governance, which provides a simple format for managing that.[57]

Without a doubt, setting the vision and priorities should involve more of the school's community than the governing board and the senior leadership team. Staff involvement is crucial in this review and development, and the final strategy agreed by the board needs to be communicated well. Many of the chapters here highlight the importance of the whole school community.

A strategy should be limited in the number of priorities if it is going to be effective, but it would be usual for an organisation's strategy to include something about the development of staff and the health of the organisation. In addition to an annual staff survey, the governing board also needs some measures to be regularly reported; these would normally include staff absence, including sickness, and staff turnover.

The framework for governance encourages schools to be innovative and imaginative in the data it is collecting – we need to try and measure what we value, not just value what is currently measured by the DfE performance tables. Although this is hard, it would be great to see more schools attempting to do this – seizing the agenda and not limiting themselves slavishly to the measures set externally. There is much more room for schools to be creative on this front than is currently being exhibited.

Of course not everything important can be boiled down to a neat mathematical equation; soft data can be as useful as hard. Schools need to try harder to achieve a balanced set of different types of measures for progress of the school which are meaningful to the school community and the outside world.

We also suggest that the board, or the relevant resources committee, gets summary

---

57 www.nga.org.uk/Guidance/Workings-Of-The-Governing-Body/Governance-Tools/ Framework-for-Governance.aspx (accessed 20 May 2016)

reports from exit interviews undertaken with staff that are leaving. That data of course will not provide answers; it needs to be compared with other schools, and is only the beginning of a conversation about what could be improved.

Holding the headteacher to account

The role of the governing board is to hold the lead executive (in this chapter I am defaulting to the term headteacher, but in multi academy trusts it will be an executive head or chief executive officer) to account for delivery of the strategic priorities, and these should involve discussions of culture, climate and leadership style. However governing boards do not always do this very well, resorting to an overriding emphasis on test and examinations results. Although clearly important, they do not tell the whole improvement story.

Those governing must not over-step the mark and begin interfering with the operations of the school. Generally governors and trustees are not of the education world, and therefore tend to stay out of educational policies but keep to their comfort zones, the areas of their own professional competency such as finances and HR. They sometimes stray from the strategic into operational, and while headteachers are sometimes very grateful for that *pro bono* help, it leads to an educational profession which does not always develop its own competence in those areas critical to managing an organisation, and a governing board which does not insist on this as it should.

On the other hand governing boards do tend to stay at the strategic level on educational issues, with the consequence that most would therefore not have had conversations about two of the subjects which have been identified as contributing greatly to teachers' workload: lesson planning and marking. They are also areas that admittedly NGA has steered away from, apart from reminders that leadership shouldn't follow diktats, or rumours of diktats, or the latest trend or fad in any unthinking fashion.

However governing boards should perhaps have picked up on these two areas of overload for teachers sooner; this could have been done by two basic tenets of good governance: ensuring we had more than one source of information and asking good questions. Many governors have been concerned about low morale of staff, but didn't always take that next step of asking what the school leadership could do to improve it. Many accepted that it was all due to Government policy and Ofsted pressures. While those two sources have clearly contributed to the problems, governors should have been asking more about whether school policy, practice and culture was contributing.

This is not a green light for governors to get involved in setting marking policies or lesson planning practice, but to ask the questions of any policy and practice: have staff been involved in setting it? What consequences will this have for workload? How will the impact of the policies be monitored?

Meaningful data

The third issue identified by the DfE survey as creating unnecessary work for teachers was data collection and management. I wholeheartedly support the principles outlined by the independent teacher workload review group set up by the DfE:

a. be streamlined

b. Be ruthless: only collect what is needed to support outcomes for children.

c. Be prepared to stop activities

d. Be aware of workload issues: consider not just how long it will take, but whether that time could be better spent on other tasks.

It is a sad indictment of where we had got to in schools that these were not simply taken as read. Of course governing boards do not want school staff to waste time creating junk data, nor for their board papers to include a digest of that phony data as evidence of pupil progress.

The report states that 'teachers need to know if pupils are on track to achieve end-of-year expectations, whether pupils are where they should be' and that 'unless there are issues of performance to address and monitor, summative data should not normally be collected more than three times a year per pupil'. This should suit the needs of governing boards too, which by the by are absent from the report, apart from a recommendation to governing boards 'not to request data in any other format than that which the school regularly and routinely presents'.

This exhortation illustrates a misunderstanding of the governance role and suggests those on the group were not aware of the very poor practice in some schools on data reporting which does need tackling. Governing boards not only are perfectly within their rights to request particular information – but could be failing in their role not to.

The report rightly highlights the need for data to be valid, but does not take that conversation further. And that is the central debate we all need to be having in the school system: what constitutes valid data on pupil attainment and progress? Rather than every individual school struggling with this, it would be useful to have a national conversation and examples of what this looks like.

Experience of governing boards is too often that internal pupil data provided during the school year does not stack up with external test and exam results. There are of course many other issues at play here, such as changes in the curriculum, but this is work we need to continue, to ensure the data we are all using at every level of the system is meaningful while not adding unnecessarily to the workload of school staff.

Performance management as a force for good

One of the ways in which governing boards hold the Headteacher to account is through performance management, including annual appraisals. (The exception is within multi academy trusts where an executive leader will performance manage the academies' Headteachers).

If a governing board has agreed the school's strategic priorities, then those are likely to be the objectives for the Headteacher, along with at least one concerning professional development. The same data used for monitoring progress against the school's priorities is likely to be relevant to the headteacher's objectives.

Within the schools sector, performance management (PM) tends to have a bad name, but it should form the backbone of deploying and developing staff well. Generally human resources practice in schools is not as good as it should be, and PM is sorely misunderstood; dislike and fear has been entrenched by the introduction of a small element of performance related pay. However PM conversations with a line manager should clarify expectations of both parties, be carried out in a supportive way and should always have CPD at its heart. See Robin Bevan's chapter for an example of how his school tries to address performance management constructively and openly.

This dialogue shouldn't wait until six month reviews, but regular one to one discussions should form an important vehicle for advice and mentoring. If the line manager isn't able to offer that themselves, they should find a way of sourcing the necessary support. Workload, without a doubt, comes within the remit of these discussions, and if the immediate line manager has no locus to solve problems raised, then this needs to be escalated to senior leaders or if a structural issue to the governing board. Similar issues may well be faced by others in the school and solutions will often come from the wider group.

Balancing the budget

Clearly one solution to the workload problem would be to have teachers teaching fewer or smaller classes, but with school funding being tighter over the next few years, this is a very unlikely scenario in many schools. Given the importance of good CPD, we will need to be innovative to ensure there is still space for it. (See Heath Monk's chapter for more about genuine professional development.) With staff costs being the lions' share of schools' budgets, governing boards will have to review staffing structures over the next couple of years along with ways in which resources might be better used; this may well require consideration of class sizes, which in turn will have an impact of workload. Any proposals should be discussed with the staff, and in some cases the law requires more formal consultation.

Staff governors

Almost all schools retain places for staff on their governing boards (although in multi academy trusts these are more likely to be on an academy committee level and not on the overarching board of trustees). We would encourage staff to put themselves forward and if successful, training on the role and responsibilities is essential. The governing board should insist on this, but if they don't, there are resources available for new governors, such as NGA's *Welcome to Governance*.

Staff governors do not represent the staff voice; all those who govern must do so by using their own personal judgement in the interests of pupils. Staff have to avoid wherever possible conflicts of interest, or declare them where they can't be avoided completely. It can also be tricky for staff to challenge senior leaders and it is good practice for another governor to act as a mentor to new members. Governing is a team activity and once a decision has been made, all the board has to get behind it, and not all of what is discussed can be shared with staff colleagues.

Another option is for staff to govern at other schools; this is excellent CPD and gives a better understanding of the role, and allows for practice to be compared between schools. This could be included in an annual appraisal or six month review discussion – I would hope your line manager would greet the suggestion with enthusiasm.

Leadership

While it is the leadership's role to ensure a healthy professional organisation which achieves, there is no single recipe for excellence. It will be specific to the school's history, community, values, ethos, aspirations, and also the passions and capabilities of its people. Although of course leaders can learn from each other, the challenge is to create and sustain leadership which works with these factors in this school. However there are some essential ingredients including, importantly, trust and respect. This needs to emanate from the relationships the governing board has, and be replicated in all parts of the school.

Schools leaders are usually not oblivious to the extent of unhappiness in their schools, but they may avoid addressing it. It is easier and less confrontational to 'lay low' with an angry culture than to take the risks associated with trying to improve it. Some headteachers may not believe that it is even possible to turn round staff morale or may not have the confidence that they are capable of bringing about a more positive culture.

Although image, techniques and skills can influence a leader's outward success, the weight of real effectiveness as a leader probably lies in good character as much as in professional competence. By good character, I mean integrity, maturity, loyalty, kindness and consistency – alongside a willingness to admit when you are wrong. These traits will help build those important trusting, considerate and respectful relationships which in turn help foster open and honest communication. It means avoiding a focus on the weaknesses of other people , or looking to blame other people and circumstances.

Leaders need to have strategies to ensure the stress they experience as a result of external pressures and constraints does not transfer to the rest of the workforce. Governing boards and particularly the chair should play an important part in this. Their role in supporting the Headteacher and acting as a sounding board is critical. Those characteristics I have just identified as necessary for the professional leadership are just as apt for those governing.

There is no formula for getting right the balance of protecting staff from the unnecessary distraction of external noise while equipping them to be a resilient flexible workforce which can adapt to change. This will be a judgement call, one a Headteacher will often discuss in advance with the chair. Generally, transparency is the best policy in developing a culture of engagement with staff, but sometimes life is more complicated and the Headteacher must decide what information is necessary to share.

There is a culture amongst some school leaders of compliance, always looking upwards to Ofsted or the Department for Education. Beware of phrases such as: 'We have to'; 'We must'; 'They won't allow that'; 'They have decided that' being resorted to as reasons for changing a system without a good explanation.

Too much of the recent practice which has caused additional stress or work for school staff appears to have been as a result of school leaders best guessing the requirements from on high; there is no other explanation for the onerous marking policies which were being used in some schools. Leadership which stands up to those external pressures requires courage.

Takeaway

Schools need to be good, vibrant places to work.

The governing board has a duty of care towards you as an employee. They need to be monitoring workload and wellbeing, and setting out plans to improve work-life balance. If your school doesn't regularly survey staff, anonymously, it's difficult (perhaps impossible) for your governing board to carry out that duty of care.

Questions

Do you know what your school's strategic priorities are? Do they include staff wellbeing and development?

Does your school survey staff on workload and well-being? Do you know how this is used by the governing board?

Have you been involved (with the governing board) in reviewing your school's vision?

Do you discuss workload in your one-to-ones and within your performance management reviews?

A quick guide to data

(taken from ATL's workload campaign)

What's the problem?

It takes too long and it's too detailed

The focus is on data entry rather than analysis

The data aren't relevant

The system we use is wrong for our purposes

'Does knowing a three year old is worth 4% help them improve?'

Should we collect and analyse data?

The Grattan Institute in Australia stated in 2015[58] that while schools are 'awash with data, many do not collect the data they really need, or use the data they do collect effectively...' It's not only schools, but the education system generally, which is drowning in data. We have got into a situation where national data takes precedence, and our efforts are put into mapping where our school data sits in relation to that.

'Data' is information. It's important to be able to reflect on what we know about the students we teach – and this extends beyond their performance in tests. It includes information about attainment and behaviour, needs and interventions, past achievements and current interests. Teachers and leaders have always done this, through markbooks, registers and behaviour logs for example. We report it to pupils and parents, and also to many other stakeholders. But its main importance should be to enable teachers to continually improve teaching, by understanding what has an impact on pupils' learning.

The trouble is that we now increasingly use the data we collect to judge whether we're meeting targets, and to crack down on those pupils and teachers who don't seem to be 'making progress'. This can lead to frequent testing and data entry, frequent analysis of tiny data sets, and a focus on small movements of numbers, which may represent a single pupil having a bad day. Data can provide important information, but should never be used as an automatic verdict on teaching, on learners or on schools.

---

58 grattan.edu.au/wp-content/uploads/2015/07/827-Targeted-Teaching.pdf particularly 'how schools and teachers can get the data they need' (p17ff)

What might good practice look like?

NFER, in a report commissioned by the DfES in 2005 explained that data 'only becomes effective if it stimulates questions about the actual learning that is taking place and how it can be developed further'.

The Commission on assessment without levels[59] suggests that teachers should ask the fundamental question: what purposes are the data intended to support?

Until you know the answer to that question, it is hard to know what data to collect, how frequently, or how to analyse and report it. Once you have agreed the purposes, then these answers become more obvious.

A school that manages data well will have a strong understanding of how to use it to identify individuals who need support. Its assessment policy will set out when it is useful to record data, and when it is not. It will also explain how the data will be analysed and what decisions and actions can be taken based on the data.

It's important that teachers can consider data collaboratively. When teachers are teaching the same children, the same subjects or the same topic over time, analysis of trends can generate useful information about what might be happening and how to support or change that. Teachers can only do this in an atmosphere of trust. Where data is used judgementally or punitively, whether by SLT or because of inspection judgements, it is much more difficult to be open about your data and to learn from it.

In 2005, the NfER reported that 'inadequate training or support resulted in staff viewing data as a threat.' Not much has changed since then for many teachers. Good practice needs to be supported by collaborative CPD, looking at how to use the data constructively, reflecting on the questions that teachers want to ask about their own practice and how to use data to answer those questions, rather than just the current focus on how to use the systems, how to interpret national data and what school data tells you about the progress your pupils made this term.

How can you make marking more manageable?

As part of the Workload challenge, the DfE has put together a working group on data, which produced recommendations in Spring 2016. The DfE response to the Workload Challenge[60] contained an appendix of useful suggestions (see page 22).

---

59 www.gov.uk/government/publications/commission-on-assessment-without-levels-final-report

60 www.gov.uk/government/uploads/system/uploads/attachment_data/file/415874/ Government_Response_to_the_Workload_Challenge.pdf

For data it suggests:

- Effective use of whole school data management system/registers (including training for staff)
- use of software for tracking pupil progress
- use of tablets for assessments
- effective use of support staff, *eg* removing administrative tasks from pupil-facing roles, sharing data managers with partner schools
- Teacher-led CPD with a focus on improving practice rather than disseminating information
- use of online tools for administrative processes.

The Ofsted clarification[61] document says:

Ofsted will take a range of evidence into account when making judgements, including published performance data, the school's in-year performance information and work in pupils' books and folders, including that held in electronic form.

Ofsted does not expect performance and pupil-tracking information to be presented in a particular format. Such information should be provided to inspectors in the format that the school would ordinarily use to monitor the progress of pupils in that school.

Who should enter data?

- Data entry is an administrative process, and could be done by dedicated admin staff
- Forms and reports could be pre-populated with as much data as possible (*eg* names and dates of birth, pupil premium status, previous attainment)

Data should be entered once and not duplicated

- It's moving data from one system to another, whether from paper to computer, or between systems, that wastes time.
- We need better systems that enable transfer from mark books.

Only collect relevant data

- Too much data is collected because we think Ofsted want it, or to report

---

61 www.gov.uk/government/uploads/system/uploads/attachment_data/file/463242/ Ofsted_inspections_clarification_for_schools.pdf

to the governors.

· Teachers need to identify what data is useful for their teaching, and ensure the systems can collect and analyse that data.

Choose a system and stick with it

Teachers and school leaders need to spend time choosing or developing an appropriate system, and then stay with that system. The system itself needs to stay stable too, as changes to the way it functions mean spending time re-learning how to use the software.

Teachers need ample notice of changes in assessment and reporting policies, with guidance available well in advance of those changes. Otherwise much time is wasted inventing a system that will be overtaken by national events.

How to cut your workload by reducing the time you spend with data

· Find someone else to enter the data.
· Only enter data once.
· Rethink how frequently you enter data.
· Rethink how often you analyse and report on data.
· Don't enter formative assessment data – you need to act on that information and there is little intrinsic value in recording it.

It is almost impossible to take these actions as an individual. Data collection and analysis is usually decided at a school or departmental level. It is important to discuss the issues with colleagues in order to find a way through the data overload.

Questions to discuss with colleagues/senior leadership

· What purposes are our data intended to support? (See Assessment without Levels commission, final report)
· Who will use and interpret the data, and how will they use it?
· What decisions or actions do we want to be able to take, based on the data?
· Are the assessments we use reliable and valid? (There's no point collecting data from poor assessments)
· Does your data help you to improve pupil learning?
· Does your data help you to reflect on your teaching? In particular to track whether a particular intervention has made a difference and to which pupils?

- How much time does it take to enter the data? It will be useful to track how long it takes so that you have collective evidence. You can then make informed arguments about whether it would be cost-effective to employ (or share) a data manager, or what other aspects of your role will need to be dropped in order to make the time for data entry/analysis.

- Do you have a member of staff with responsibility for leading data analysis? The NFER report suggests that 'useful discussions of data amongst staff tended to occur in schools where one person took a proactive role in using data to move learning forward.'

- How frequently should you record summative assessment data? The Commission on assessment without levels says that 'Recording summative data more frequently than three times a year is not likely to provide useful information'.

- Can you evaluate the systems you use to collect and analyse data? Useful questions for this would be:
    - Does the product support the school's policy on assessment?
    - To what extent will it support delivery of that policy?
    - Is the assessment approach implied by the product credible? (In particular the Commission points out that systems which dictate formative assessment may not be right for your situation)
    - Does the product provide good value?

- What training do you need in order to understand how best to use the data to support your practice, and how best to collect data that answers the questions you want to raise?

- Does your assessment or data policy include information about when it is necessary to record assessment data, and how to manage the workload implications?

More haste, less speed: the impact of government policy on teacher workload

Mary Bousted

It is an interesting fact that some jurisdictions with, shall we say, more stable electoral mandates, such as Shanghai and Singapore, regularly top the PISA international league tables.

There will, of course, be a complex interplay of reasons for the educational success of these jurisdictions but one hugely significant factor in the success or failure of national education reform is the way in which it is managed; the timescale in which it is implemented, and the support given to the teachers and school leaders who are required to do new things in different ways.

The frenetic pace of change

In England, electoral terms of four and five years and frequent changes of education ministers have launched repeated waves of policy initiative upon ranks of weary teachers. These have encompassed every area of their work – from how they should teach, to the seemingly never ending creation of new types of school. Having vacated the field of industrial policy, and only recently having re-discovered a penchant for regional policy, ministers have focused their attention on public policy. Education and health, the biggest and most costly public services, have been seen by ambitious politicians as the place to make their mark.

In this endeavour they have been enthusiastically supported by the media, which loves a good story and is a hungry beast that needs feeding on a daily basis. This leaves the politicians with a problem. The party machine, driven by the No 10 press office, wants a steady stream of media announcements to 'fill the grid' – the pre-planned press notices which every administration needs to generate to demonstrate that it is running the country determinedly and decisively.

Headlines of plummeting educational standards support the cry that 'something must be done'. Often these invoke war-like images. Education ministers are 'doing battle', 'winning the war', 'fighting' poor discipline, plummeting literacy and/or numeracy standards, the childhood obesity epidemic (to give just a taste of the many and varied battles waged by education ministers). Caught in the cross fire are teachers and school leaders who are made to feel responsible for societal issues which they can do little to control. All too often those same professionals, wearied by constant criticism and constant change, required to implement the next thing, and then the next, hang up their teaching and school leadership boots for a life less stressful.

Politicians rarely pause to consider the cumulative effect of their constant attacks on the profession. This is an issue I have raised repeatedly with government education ministers who reply, plaintively, that they do make positive statements about schools and teachers. This is true. They do. But a positive sentence or two at the start of a ministerial speech is quickly followed by paragraphs of detailed critique – some of it justified – and the effect is imbalanced. And there is nothing, it seems, that the press loves more than headlines screaming that standards are plummeting, and that something must be done.

Whether policies announced with huge media fanfare prove to be successful or otherwise, they rarely get the same media attention. It usually takes years to determine whether or not a policy intervention has been successful. Journalists have short memories and the frenetic pace of the media, intensified by the advent of social media, leaves little time or space for reflection and evaluation. This is where Shanghai, and Singapore, and other nations with, let us say, more permanent governments appear to have a clear advantage. Their ministers are not expected to announce a weekly education initiative. A more compliant media enables education policy to be enacted on a different timescale; to be long term (usually decades) and to be carefully evaluated throughout the implementation period. All of which are essential pre-requisites of effective education policy making.

Policy-making for the long term

Policy makers looking to implement effective education policy should resist, at all costs, the urge (and it is a powerful political urge) to look forward to a rosy past. Andreas Schleicher, the Division Head and coordinator of the OECD Programme for International Student Assessment (PISA) and the OECD Indicators of Education Systems programme, makes the case for forward looking education policy very convincingly when he writes:

Today's teacher needs to prepare students for jobs that have not yet been created, to use technologies that have not yet been invented, and to solve social problems that haven't arisen before. Teachers have to do more than transmit educational content; they have to cultivate students' ability to be creative, think critically, solve problems and make decisions; they have to build students' capacity to recognise and exploit the potential of new technologies; and they have to nurture the character qualities that help people to live and work together.

Schleicher outlines what are the essential elements of effective political intervention in a nation's education system. He considers clarity of purpose to be the foundation of successful education policy making and argues that, above all, there should be close alignment between national education policy objectives and the learning objectives that schools are required to achieve.[62]

Politicians and policy makers should, Schleicher argues, strive for consensus about education reform. They need to communicate a long term vision of what is to be accomplished for student learning and engage stakeholders, especially teachers, in formulating and implementing policy responses, without compromising the drive for improvement.

Finding time for reform

Reforming educational policy-makers must understand that teachers and school leaders do not possess unlimited amounts of time to implement new initiatives. They already have more than a full time job doing their current work in schools and classrooms.

Reducing teacher and school leader bureaucratic workload should be a central plank of policy reform in education, something which Nicky Morgan, then Secretary of State for Education, realised and which led to her launching the workload challenge, asking teachers about the drivers for excessive workload. It is now the case that teachers and school leaders work more unpaid overtime than any other profession.

I have spoken and written about the terrible effects of teacher workload on many occasions. Teachers are not shirkers. They don't mind hard work. They do, however, mind unproductive, busy work which does nothing to improve their teaching or advance their pupils' learning.

The majority of the madly excessive workload which is driving teachers at all stages of their career from the profession is not focused on improving teaching or learning, but on recording what teachers do – as though nothing is done, no differentiation, no assessment for learning, no group work, nothing unless it is written down. As the earlier chapters in this book demonstrate, the government's workload challenge has identified this as the driver of unnecessary workload, and has tried to set out some ways of addressing it.

---

62 Andreas Schleicher (2016) *Teaching Excellence through Professional Learning and Policy Reform*, OECD p.9

What really makes a difference; building teacher professionalism

Policy-makers should prioritise the activities that have the greatest impact on teachers' practices, and should prioritise building teacher professionalism. In particular, they and the profession must establish clearly and concisely what teachers are expected to know and be able to do. On this basis of a shared understanding of teacher professionalism, initial and ongoing teacher training and continuing professional development should be built. The expectation should be for teachers to be life-long learners with initial teacher training providing the foundation for continuing, ongoing learning.

If teachers are to have self-efficacy and motivation, then they must feel empowered in their work and possess a strong sense of professional agency. Successful policy implementation requires teachers who feel 'done with' rather than 'done to' and teachers should be included in decision making at school level, and beyond.

It is my view, however, gained from talking to teachers and their representatives, and from debates at ATL's national conference and in its Executive committee, that schools are becoming less collaborative and more compliant places to work, and that accountability pressures, and in particular the drive to satisfy what school leaders conceive to be Ofsted's requirements, lead to practices which undermine and constrain teacher efficacy and motivation. Under pressure, the temptation for school leaders is command and control mode. And whilst this is sometimes a necessary stage to initiate and drive change, it has severe defects as a long term management tool.

AMIE, ATL's leadership section, strongly promotes the value that schools gain when school leaders devise systems to recognise and promote teachers – growing their own leadership development within the school. Central to this endeavour is the provision of career tracks to enable teachers to confidently take on positions of responsibility in the school, and providing opportunities for leadership training and development of all the staff in the school at all levels.

School leaders who recognise that their staff are their most precious resource (particularly at a time where the majority of European countries are experiencing a teacher shortage) are ideally placed to demonstrate, through practical measures, that they value their colleagues' opinions and professional expertise and that their school is a positive, productive place to work. School leaders who do not display this awareness, and have not taken the steps to promote staff well-being and professional respect, will find it increasingly difficult, in a very challenging teacher recruitment market, to recruit teachers.

Reducing in-school variation of teacher quality

One of the most productive ways to ensure higher educational standards within schools, regionally and nationally, is to reduce in-school variation of teaching quality. The UK education system has one of the highest levels of variation in student outcomes within the OECD; as much as 80 per cent of the variation in achievement among UK students lies within schools, four times more than that which occurs between different schools. And the problem gets worse the longer pupils are in school – at Key Stage 2, in-school variation is five times greater than between-school variance; for Key Stage 4 it is fourteen times greater.

Given the fact of, and effect of, in-school variation of teaching quality, one would think that this would be a major area for policy-makers to consider. Too often, however, it is not on their horizons. That is because, when it gets down to the detail of the practice of accomplished and effective teaching, the media loses interest. Headlines are not made of such stuff. But this is where the real gains are to be made by policy-makers.

No education system can exceed the quality of its teachers. Everyone, it seems, agrees with that mantra. The problem is that the conditions required to support teacher professional growth and development are, too often, not adequately considered by policy makers, nor are the resources devoted, at government level, to provide career long, high quality, professional development for teachers and school leaders.

Learning together

One of the best ways to tackle in-school variation of teaching quality is to provide the opportunity for teachers to learn from one another. School leaders should strengthen peer collaboration through induction programmes and mentoring; through peer observation which is formative and does not result in a grade or number designating the 'quality' of the observed lesson which will, much more often than not, be inaccurate.

Policy-makers would do well to consider how best teachers within, and across, schools can share best practice and should ask themselves the fundamental question: how can inter-school collaboration and cooperation, leading to shared professional learning, flourish? How can the time be created for this important work? What are the mechanisms which would support this, and what are the means to evaluate it?

There is one more point to make about teacher and school leaders' continuing professional development which is this: it cannot be done on the cheap.

Policy reform needs to be accompanied by long term, sustainable and adequate financing. I am sorry to say that this is rarely the case. Politicians wish for the moon in education terms but almost never provide the rockets for the teaching profession to make a landing. In years of negotiations with civil servants at the Department for Education, and with government ministers, the issue of an entitlement for all teachers to access good quality, professionally relevant CPD has been repeatedly kicked into the long grass – something that is regarded as desirable, and necessary to improve standards, but not achievable at that particular point in the political cycle. Yet there is no more effective way of developing higher educational standards than to invest in initial teacher training and continuing professional development, and such an investment grows ever more necessary as teachers are in ever shorter supply.

Teacher retention in the profession is now as great a problem as teacher recruitment. Last year, in England, over 50,000 teachers, 11% of the profession, left before retirement. This is a huge, and growing problem – a wasted resource at a time where pupil numbers are rising.

Politicians must recognise, above all, that they cannot sustain constant policy churn – new curricula, new qualifications, new teaching standards and so on and so on – without giving teachers and school leaders the professional development which will enable them to rise to the challenge of change, and without removing the policies and practices that add unnecessary 'busywork'.

Reforming education policy-making

All of the above leads me to conclude that education policy reform is neither easy nor quick. This is a vital lesson for policy-makers to learn if they are to stop the damaging increases to teacher workload. Andreas Schleicher argues that it is rarely possible to predict clear, identifiable links between education policies and outcomes, 'especially given the lag involved between the time at which the initial cost of reform is incurred and the time when it is evident whether the intended benefits of reforms actually materialise.'[63]

Added to this is the large number of variables which make it very difficult to identify links between policies and their outcomes and it is not difficult to understand why there is so much political debate and disagreement over the outcomes of previously implemented education policies.

---

63 Schleicher, A (2016) Teaching Excellence through Professional Learning and Policy Reform, OECD p3

But time for reflection is vital if we are to move away from policy-churn which increases the unnecessary, often short term, workload for teachers and leaders.

I finish with one final, but important, truth, which is that teachers are more trusted and valued by the public than politicians. Any resistance to education policy reform by teachers is likely to be at least partially effective. So it makes great political sense to do everything possible to get the teaching profession 'on board', early on, in policy thinking and planning. More haste, less speed, should be the notice above every education minister's desk.

Takeaway

There is no more effective way of improving education standards than investing in ITT and CPD.

Politicians who aim for the quick fix are part of the problem, not the solution. Politicians and policy-makers need to engage the profession if change is to be sustainable.

Questions

What one national policy change would make the biggest difference to your work?

Have you ever contacted your MP about these issues? Or your union?

How could teachers (you) get involved in policy thinking and planning? How could you feel less 'done to' and more 'done with'?

Do you know how your union engages in these debates?

Conclusion

Each of these chapters reminds us that tackling workload is not a once-and-forever task, but one that must be continually at the front of your mind.

First, there are things that you can stop doing. You need to work those out in your school context, and it may not be straightforward – but this is a powerful first step.

There are things we all need to do better – whether that means finding more efficient ways to do things, or more collaborative, more reflective, more evidence-based ways of doing things (hopefully, always evidence-based). You will probably need to engage with colleagues and leaders, and look externally, if these changes are to happen, and to be sustained.

But it's not all down to individuals or groups in schools. Government also has a responsibility to do things better. To bring about change where it matters – particularly in teacher education and professional development. And to stop making large-scale changes at speed, which undermine all that a school is trying to do.

Although it doesn't always feel like it, we can influence government and its agencies. On your own, you can make some changes. Collectively we can change a lot more.

Teaching is the kind of job where there's always one more thing you could do, that would make your teaching, your lesson, your reports, even better. But when you choose to do something, you also choose not to do something else. That 'something else' could be a focus on yourself, your health, your family; it could be taking some space to be creative and reignite your excitement about teaching. Do you know what will have the bigger impact?

If we only had the time, we could really work together to make changes that count. It's surely our responsibility to make the time: I hope this book helps you to do exactly that.